INDUSTRIAL PUBLICITY

WILEY SERIES ON HUMAN COMMUNICATION
Kenneth G. Tong, Editor

W. A. Mambert
PRESENTING TECHNICAL IDEAS: A Guide to Audience Communication

William J. Bowman
GRAPHIC COMMUNICATION

Herman M. Weisman
TECHNICAL CORRESPONDENCE: A Handbook and Reference Source for the Technical Professional

John H. Mitchell
WRITING FOR TECHNICAL AND PROFESSIONAL JOURNALS

James J. Welsh
THE SPEECH WRITING GUIDE: Professional Techniques for Regular and Occasional Speakers

Michael P. Jaquish
PERSONAL RESUME PREPARATION

George T. Vardaman and Carroll C. Halterman
COMMUNICATION FOR MANAGERIAL CONTROL: Systems for Organizational Diagnosis and Design

John D. Haughney
EFFECTIVE CATALOGS

Robert H. Dodds
WRITING FOR TECHNICAL AND BUSINESS MAGAZINES

George A. Magnan
USING TECHNICAL ART: An Industry Guide

Milton Feinberg
TECHNIQUES OF PHOTOJOURNALISM

John B. Bennett
EDITING FOR ENGINEERS

George T. Vardaman, Carroll C. Halterman, and Patricia Black Vardaman
CUTTING COMMUNICATION COSTS AND INCREASING IMPACTS

Stello Jordan (Editor)
HANDBOOK OF TECHNICAL PRACTICES, in two volumes

John M. Stormes and James P. Crumpler
TELEVISION COMMUNICATIONS SYSTEMS FOR BUSINESS AND INDUSTRY

Harold E. Daubert
INDUSTRIAL PUBLICITY

INDUSTRIAL PUBLICITY

HAROLD E. DAUBERT

A WILEY-INTERSCIENCE PUBLICATION

JOHN WILEY & SONS

New York • London • Sydney • Toronto

Copyright © 1974, by John Wiley & Sons, Inc.

All rights reserved. Published simultaneously in Canada.

No part of this book may be reproduced by any means, nor transmitted, nor translated into a machine language without the written permission of the publisher.

Library of Congress Cataloging in Publication Data:

Daubert, Harold E   1934–
  Industrial publicity.

  (Wiley series on human communication)
  "A Wiley-Interscience publication."
  1. Public relations. I. Title.

HD59.D33   659.2   74-1043
ISBN 0-471-19640-1

Printed in the United States of America

10-9 8 7 6 5 4 3 2 1

PREFACE

When I entered public relations work 13 years ago, I was at first surprised and then frustrated by what seemed to me to be a scarcity of practical advice in the field's literature. That, along with a compulsion to write, is the main reason for publication of this volume.

To keep the book on a practical level, I have focused on the methods of planning, producing, and disseminating industrial publicity in support of both public relations and marketing objectives. They are sometimes the same, but there are distinctions between the two which industrial executives sometimes do not recognize.

The chapters that follow are based on my research and experience, and on knowledge absorbed from others I have worked with over the years in the industrial communications fields. The book does not necessarily reflect the views of the company for which I work, but is an amalgam of ideas, approaches, and methods that in my opinion seem sensible and effective.

The intended readers of the book include practicing and potential public relations practitioners, corporation and agency executives and specialists and students of industrial communications.

Most books on public relations do not explain very well how it relates to advertising and other tools of industrial communications. I have written this from the industrial communications viewpoint.

The first part of the book, Chapters 1 through 5, describes industrial publicity, the need for it, how it fits in a corporation's communications program, and the industrial and publishing environments in which it operates. The remaining chapters detail the practical application of publicity techniques, with stress on the planning function and the relation of publicity to other communications methods.

HAROLD E. DAUBERT

Washington, D.C.
November 1973

CONTENTS

INDUSTRIAL PUBLICITY

1
INDUSTRIAL PUBLICITY
IN PERSPECTIVE

THE ROOTS OF INDUSTRIAL PUBLICITY

Scholars have traced the roots of publicity all the way back to the earliest civilizations. They have found that in the United States it was used as early as the American Revolution by Samuel Adams and his associates to help their cause. The next major use was during Andrew Jackson's presidency. A member of Jackson's Kitchen Cabinet, Amos Kendall, was the president's strategist and publicist.

The first significant use of *industrial* publicity in the United States came in the late 1800s and early 1900s as a reaction to the waves of protest and reform caused by the excesses of the robber barons and their imitators. But the real groundwork of modern publicity, industrial and other, was laid during World War I by the Committee on Public Information. This group was established by President Wilson on the suggestion of George Creel, a journalist friend and supporter of Wilson. The far-reaching effects of the committee were described by Mock and Larsen in *Words That Won the War*:

> Mr. Creel assembled as brilliant and talented a group of journalists, scholars, press agents, editors, artists, and other manipulators of the symbols of public opinion as America had ever seen united for a single purpose. It was a gargantuan advertising agency the like of which the country had never known, and the breathtaking scope of its activities was not to be equalled until the rise of the totalitarian dictatorships after the war.

Some of the practitioners, such as George Creel, Carl Byoir, Edgar Sission, Harvey Higgins, and Guy Stanton Ford, who received their training on the Creel committee carried new-found knowledge into industrial publicity work after the war. Edward L. Bernays, one of the pioneers in the

1

field, said, "1919–1929 saw the introduction of large-scale industrial publicity. This stems in part from principles and practices successfully tested and proven in the Great War."

The events stemming from the catastrophic depression of 1929 and Franklin D. Roosevelt's New Deal showed the necessity for building public support. The social and economic upheavals of the depression were barely over when violent change came again, in the form of World War II. Once again the United States government mounted an information program, this time under the newly formed Office of War Information headed by Elmer Davis. This effort dwarfed the World War I Creel committee in size and scope. New publicity techniques were developed and tested, and many new specialists were trained. Again, many of them wound up in industry.

No major upsurges in the "technology" of industrial publicity have occurred since World War II, but there has been a steady growth of its use since.

INFLUENCE OF CHANGE

The changes that have occurred in the world since the beginning of the industrial revolution have forced industry to evolve from the simple laissez faire way of doing business. There was a time when a company could make and sell its products in a seller's market and could afford to have a "public be damned" attitude. The forces of change have caused a gradual reversal of that attitude.

Changes occur at a bewildering rate. They have made it ever more difficult and complicated to do business. For some companies, especially small concerns, priorities have shifted from maximizing profits to simple survival. And survival is tied to communication more than ever before.

There are multitudes of causes for the changes and their multiplying effects. There are also many different ways of looking at the causes. One way is from the social viewpoint. Some of the social factors are population growth, broader education, urbanization, mobility, and shifts in the proportion of young and old people. Higher living standards have led to higher expectations on the part of the public; being better informed has led to a more selective public.

From the political viewpoint, the proliferation of laws, rulings, and regulations, and the extension of government power in general, have played a strong role in the shaping of change in our society.

In the industrial environment, the shift from a production-oriented to a consumption-oriented economy was a significant factor. Labor unions of course played an important part. Changing patterns of industrial operation and expansion also entered in. These include the push toward diversified, conglomerate, multinational corporations. Sheer size and complexity resulting from the growth tendency have led to anonymity and alienation among workers and even bosses.

Size, complexity, and modern management methods have resulted in what John Kenneth Galbraith, in the *New Industrial State*, refers to as the "technostructure," an army of unknown specialists, mostly in the ranks of middle management, who make decisions, usually by committee and often anonymously.

New scientific knowledge applied to practical problems by engineering—in a word, technology—has had an increasingly important influence on change. According to Alvin Toffler, in *Future Shock*, technological advance is "the critical node in the network of causes; indeed, it may be the node that activates the entire net."

One very important side effect of technological advance is what has been called the information explosion. Toffler notes: "Today change is so swift and relentless that yesterday's truths become today's fictions, and the most highly skilled and intelligent members of society admit difficulty in keeping up with the deluge of new knowledge—even in extremely narrow fields." The proliferation of new information is the main reason for the torrent of messages vying for the attention of the public.

In light of the information explosion, one necessary ingredient for success in industry is to be able to obtain, process, and disseminate information in a highly effective manner.

But the information explosion is just a side effect, and powerful mainstream effects have brought us to where we are today.

In the early days of the industrial revolution, the economic system was far and away the most important controlling force in our society. Events since then have made political and social influences as important as economic ones. Industry has been slow in responding to political and social forces. This has caused vague discontentment which has in the recent past crystallized as consumerism and environmentalism.

Industry has also received most of the blame for inflation. At first glance, this may seem illogical. But the reason is simply that the manufacturer is the one who ultimately jacks up the price. Higher costs to the consumer may be due to any number of factors such as lower worker productivity, high wage settlements, new government controls, or world economic effects on raw material costs. But a producer who raises the price on a product that bears his name is the one who feels the brunt of public disfavor.

Public alarm resulting from consumerism, environmentalism, inflation, and other causes has led to new heights of skepticism and even outright hostility toward industry. As a result, there is increasing pressure on industrial management to pay more attention to its social responsibilities.

Thomas W. Benham, president of Opinion Research Corporation, summed it up neatly in the following excerpt from a speech at the White House Conference on the Industrial World Ahead, February 6–9, 1972.

As we have seen, business must stem a flood tide of adverse public opinion if it is to continue to prosper. The business community must educate in those areas where half truths dwell and must hold itself accountable in those areas where it has fallen down in its responsibilities. The public will no longer accept lip service on pressing issues. Large numbers see their air becoming poisoned, their water undrinkable, their quality of life deteriorating. Large numbers see—and badly exaggerate—unequal distribution of wealth, hunger and poverty in the richest nation in the world, housing unfit for human habitation. Large numbers feel cheated on what they purchase, see products judged unsafe, experience poor quality, and the like.

Business must, by its deeds and words, correct these basic feelings of suspicion and resentment about its contributions to American life. If business-men fail in this, the areas of decision within which business will be able to operate will be shrunk smaller and smaller. Already the government is partner in many of your business decisions. The government's voice will grow louder and more insistent, and that of business will be reduced. There is perhaps nothing more urgent than this tremendous problem of public dissatisfaction when we lay plans to grow and expand to meet the needs of American society in the future.

The recent upsurge in public dissatisfaction with industry is not a completely new problem. But it dramatically illustrates the importance of public attitudes toward industry.

Sets of attitudes likely to affect a company's business are thought of as the concern's image.

THE UBIQUITOUS IMAGE

The word "image" has been used so much and with so many connotations that it has lost much of its meaning. It is, however, the word that best describes the way people look at organizations and institutions. The sense of the word runs through its dictionary definition in entries such as: "a mental picture of something; conception; idea; impression; symbol; embodiment; a picture or likeness of a person constructed in the unconscious and remaining there; to picture in the mind; imagine."

In *Future Shock*, Toffler offers some new insights into the meaning of image. He says that people and organizations have a kind of collective public image. He asserts that this public image "is the weighted aggregate of private (inner) images in the society." He goes on to say that these inner images are filed in the mental models of individuals and that there are thousands of such images in each mental model. They are symbols of reality and are the result of external stimuli and mental abstraction. A mental model is something people actively construct and reconstruct from moment to moment. Images are constantly being accepted, compared, associated, cross-referenced, repositioned, and discarded.

So it appears that the concept of the company image is not such a simple thing. John F. Budd, Jr., in *An Executive Primer on Public Relations*, points out, "Companies do not have single identities. Each group important to a company has its own perspectives, colored by individual viewpoints, attitudes and motivations. The sum of all these is the mosaic that represents what is generally called the 'corporate image.' " He gives a typical set of groups that might have independent images. It includes the financial community, industry, stockholders, government, employees, the local community, customers, and suppliers.

Two extremes which can define the approach a company uses in "shaping" its image are the "open-end" and "closed-end" concepts. Burt Zollo, in *The Dollars and Sense of Public Relations*, describes this concept in terms of whether a company restricts itself to serving a single industry, or is diversified. In the closed-end case, a single-industry company aims a large part of its effort at a narrow, well-defined group. At the open-end extreme, a company's efforts are not as focused, but are more general and institutional. Companies with many divisions use the open-end approach to shape their corporate image. One important complication in using this approach, however, is the necessity to achieve broad recognition which will enhance the identities of the divisions without confusing their individual publics.

A significant side effect of a good external image is that it has some positive internal effects. Employees feel better about their company if it has a good image. If the company has an image of excellence and innovation, it encourages employees to do their best and to be creative. Other side effects are that a good image attracts capable people as employees and helps a company maintain its relations with the community in which it is located.

An extremely important characteristic of the image is that it is highly subject to change. One reason is that an image changes as the company changes. Another is that events largely outside the company's control can cause its image to change drastically. A striking example of this is the effect consumerism has had on the reputations of automobile companies.

It is an ironic fact of life that building a positive image is usually a slow, arduous process, but that a bad image can be obtained overnight. The reason is that people naturally feel that others should do what is expected of them without special reward. But if others *don't* do what is expected of them, they are open to criticism.

Although an image can be built or reinforced, it cannot be manufactured. In the long run, what others think of a company is very much dependent on the attitudes and policies of the firm's leadership.

Image building can be considered the maintaining or reinforcing of positive recognition, and the modifying of negative recognition. Positive recognition is a condition of acceptability. This in turn shows itself as a predisposition to decide to do something, such as buy a product, invest in stock, or permit some action to be taken.

When a company wants to make a customer of someone who has a positive predisposition, it has the added problem of identifying a product or service to the individual.

Ideally, industry's approach to public attitudes should be to try to shape these attitudes to fit reality. And in most cases, this is what today's industrial managers try to do. They try to run their companies as good citizens as well as good businessmen. Then they try to obtain recognition for their good works.

Unfortunately, doing business is not simple enough to allow an industrial manager to make decisions that are always clearly for the good of society as well as his company. An outstanding example occurs when economic conditions, the loss of a major contract, or some other catastrophic event forces a company to lay off employees just to stay in business. Keeping the company solvent may be good for everyone in the long term, but it is hard to convince those laid off, or the community affected, that it is good for society.

So there are many instances in which the social value of a decision may be questionable, relative, or even impossible to determine. In such cases, executives must do what appears best and try to make the best interpretation of it, even though this interpretation may be called into question. This is one of the prices of being in business.

In today's world, the social value of a company's activities and its profits are related. People react to the way a company maintains its plant, helps its community, and treats its employees. How they react determines to some extent or another how well the company does. Arjay R. Miller, president of Ford, was quoted in *Advertising Age,* November 13, 1967, by E. B. White as saying, "I think that we in management cannot discharge our long-run responsibilities to shareholders unless we also behave responsibly with regard to customers, employees, government, education, the press. Acceptance of this broader responsibility is good business as well as good citizenship."

Most companies have arrived at or are moving toward the realization that in most cases it may not be possible to operate for very long at a profit without a reasonable amount of public good will. This is especially true for companies selling directly to consumers. But with new emphasis on environmental quality, new standards of safety, and ever closer scrutiny of business by government, it is true also for companies selling to industry, business, or the government.

THE ROLE OF INDUSTRIAL PUBLICITY

Industrial publicity as a specialized form of business communication has proved to be essential in today's business world. The main reason is the ever-increasing difficulty of conveying a company's message to its audience.

Some of the reasons for difficulties in communication were indicated above in the discussion on the influence of change. Even more basic, however, is the influence of human nature. The psychological makeup of people includes such elements as territorial and survival instincts, and the need for ego gratification. This causes them to be initially distrustful of others, and at times concerned with their own affairs to the point of indifference toward others. These characteristics are present in varying degrees in different people and in the same person at different times. So the starting point for communication is somewhere between the indifference stemming from egoism and the hostility due to territorial and survival instincts.

When the characteristics of human nature are considered together with the effects of acculturation in a complex industrial society, communication is seen as a formidable problem.

Throughout most of man's history, the manufacturer—a craftsman—was able to communicate face-to-face with his customers. This is of course no longer the case for virtually all of modern industry. Still, industry is faced with the necessity of somehow conveying messages about itself and its products to the people it wants as friends and customers. The development of industrial communications was a necessary consequence, and industrial publicity was developed as one of its tools.

Industrial publicity depends for its existence on the need for communication. But it also depends for its existence on the media. Budd states, "Business today exists in a nation that boasts some 10,000 newspapers, 8000 magazines, 7000 radio and tv stations, publishes millions of books a year, broadcasts some 1500 hours of news a year, and puts some 7 million words on the wires to news media every day."

Definition and Purpose

The term industrial publicity is used to describe both the field or specialization and the material that is produced or results from the efforts of industrial publicity specialists. One authority, George Black, in *Planned Industrial Publicity*, points out, "Current literature can be cited to prove that industrial publicity is everything from straight press agentry to the very essence of public relations." Having said that, however, he goes on to define it. "Industrial publicity is the arm of sales and management activity responsible for securing editorial space or time, as divorced from paid space or time, in all media read, viewed or heard by a company's customers and prospects, for the specific purpose of adding to company prestige and assisting in the meeting of sales goals."

Since definitions often mean different things to different people, it may be useful to give another explanation. Here is one that appeared in the July 1963 issue of *Western Electronic News*, a technical magazine which no longer exists. The editor said,

Publicity is news, sent by companies to editors for impartial evaluation. If the editor agrees that the subject is news, he includes it in his publication. If it isn't news, he includes it in his wastebasket. Publicity is news only when it is timely, brief, honest, and important. Publicity is not "free advertising." It is not a "commercial" for a product or a company. It is never, never a rehash of something previously submitted. Almost all technical publications are hungry for good stories about new products, processes, or services.

The two viewpoints reflected by these different explanations are both important. The first definition is from the viewpoint of industry. It reflects the industry approach of deliberately using publicity to help advance its own goals. The second definition is from the viewpoint of publications which say that if publicity is not news it is of no value to them. So industrial publicity must reconcile the two views if it is to be effective.

The meaning of publicity perhaps can be boiled down to this: It is both purposeful and newsworthy. Looking at it from industry's viewpoint, it must be conceived and designed to accomplish some definite objective, whether it be as general as image building or as specific as promoting a product. Looking at it from the viewpoint of publications, industrial publicity must be newsworthy or it will not be used.

Newsworthiness depends on the degree of interest on the part of one or more audiences. If no one is interested in a story or message, it is not newsworthy.

The degree of interest varies from subject to subject, and from audience to audience. So it is extremely important to know which audiences are to be reached and what interests them.

Important Publicity Considerations

One of the main considerations is the audience. This was touched upon in the section on image, and is treated in some detail in Chapter 7. But it may be a good idea to delve into it here somewhat to help put it in context. First of all, audiences are simply groups of people. Individuals are members of more than one audience or group. Some examples of audiences are customers, employees, educators, students, prospective employees, government officials and workers, the community in which a company is located or headquartered, and the financial world.

Audiences can be defined in a variety of ways. Here are some of them: occupation, population, sex, income, political affiliation, religion, ethnic group, region.

One group that can be considered the primary audience is that made up of editors and newsmen. They are extremely important because they decide whether or not a company's story is legitimate and newsworthy. If it is, they consider writing or publishing it.

Continuing good relations with editors and newsmen are very important. It is not that they can be bought or that they play favorites. But it is human nature for people to think more kindly of those they know. If they also respect those they know, it is another big plus. The key to obtaining this respect is confidence built upon honesty and integrity.

Another very important consideration in using publicity is planning. Its value is underscored by the fact that both Chapters 6 and 7 are devoted to it. Good planning assures that objectives are defined, and a publicity program developed around them. It also assures that the message is relevant, significant, and concise; the dissemination of the message takes place in the right way at the right time; and the message reaches the right audiences.

The main element in good planning is the objectives. In order for the objectives to be applicable and properly defined, management has to communicate its company and marketing objectives directly to the planners. If publicity objectives are adequately defined, the target audiences will be apparent or implied. Specific subjects for messages, and the way they have to be structured and delivered, will also become apparent.

The planning should take into account not only what should be done, but evaluation of the results as well. This means that the objectives should be defined in a way that permits results to be measured. That is not always possible, but should definitely be a goal. The main reason for this is the intangible nature of publicity. Anything that can be done to help show how publicity fits into the overall company scheme of things is a real asset.

Another important consideration is the recognition that publicity has limitations. It usually cannot be expected to accomplish the entire communications job by itself. Two of the main limitations, competition and lack of newsworthiness, are illustrated by Zollo when he says that city editors receive approximately 250 press releases a day and use from 5 to 20 percent of them. This means that, at best, they use only one-fifth of the releases. From 80 to 95 percent are wastebasketed.

Competition affects the proportion of press releases used. The sheer number of stories from companies, agencies, and consultants amounts to more material than could possibly be used. Space is simply not available. Lack of newsworthiness is also a factor. If a press release says nothing of significance, it will not be used even if the space is available.

The subject of newsworthiness is explored in some depth in succeeding chapters, especially in Chapter 11. Its importance cannot be overemphasized. People in industry, particularly marketeers who have a high opinion of their wares, often fail to understand the significance of the element of news. Since they are so close to their own products and companies, they feel that newsmen and editors cannot help but share their enthusiasm. But there is a distinction between dispensing news and dispensing information based solely on the feeling that one's products and company are better than others.

Another important publicity consideration is the cost of implementing it. "In-house" expenses include salaries, office space and services and supplies, payroll and other administration, travel, entertainment, clipping services, photography, reproduction, and postage. If a company uses an outside agency or consultant, that is of course an added expense.

Just to give an idea of the magnitude of the cost of external services, counseling firms charge hourly rates ranging from about $25 to $100 per hour. The cost of a single publicity project might run from $200 to $2000. Using a consultant or counseling firm the equivalent of one professional full-time for a year might cost $50,000.

So publicity is not free. But if it is planned properly and performed professionally, it is a bargain.

REFERENCES

George Black, *Planned Industrial Publicity*, Putnam Publishing Company, Chicago, Ill., 1952.

John F. Budd, Jr., *An Executive's Primer on Public Relations*, Chilton Book Company, Philadelphia, Pa., 1969.

Scott M. Cutlip and Allen H. Center, *Effective Public Relations*, 4th ed., Prentice-Hall, Inc., Englewood Cliffs, N.J., 1971.

Bernadette W. Hoyle, *Information Services in Public Welfare Agencies*, WA Publication 19, Welfare Administration, U.S. Dept. of Health, Education and Welfare, U.S. Government Printing Office, Washington, D.C., 1960.

Raymond Simon, Ed., *Perspective in Public Relations*, University of Oklahoma Press, Norman, Okla., 1966.

Alvin Toffler, *Future Shock*, Random House, Inc., New York, N.Y., 1970.

Burt Zollo, *The Dollars and Sense of Public Relations*, McGraw-Hill Book Company, New York, N.Y., 1967.

2
IS PUBLICITY MANAGED NEWS?

This chapter touches on some large questions that cannot possibly be answered in a treatment as short as this must be—if they can be answered at all. Its purpose is just to give a flavor of some of the larger considerations that impinge upon the practice of industrial publicity. This hopefully will be of use in making sound planning decisions.

NEWS MANAGEMENT

Everyone who becomes involved in publicity, either from the using or from the receiving end, at some time or another becomes concerned about its ethics. Terms such as news management and, especially, propaganda are bothersome to many people. What follows in this chapter is intended to clarify this emotionally loaded issue and hopefully ameliorate some of the uneasiness it may cause.

To put it as bluntly and honestly as possible, industrial publicity does in a large sense use news management, which is the issuing of selected news to help meet some company objective. And to make matters worse, news management is considered by many as no more than a modern euphemism for propaganda.

Propaganda

Although the word propaganda is by definition neutral, most of us feel it has a negative connotation and implies falsification and trickery. This attitude is due partly to simple distrust and partly to the all too familiar use of propaganda in psychological warfare, especially during and since World War II. And in the final analysis, in the worst sense of the word, propaganda can be unpleasant and even immoral.

But there is another side to propaganda, which is exemplified by the word's roots. It is a Latin word defined as propagation in the sense of

12

making known or spreading ideas and customs. It seems to have been coined in the seventeenth century. The Roman Catholic Church formed its Sacra Congregation de Propaganda Fide (Sacred Congregation for Propagating the Faith) which became known simply as the Propaganda. Now this is not intended to mean that propaganda is good just because it is used by organized religion, but simply to show that it can be used with good intentions as well as bad.

It is remarkably easy to become mired in a bog of semantics when trying to consider objectively an abstract concept—like propaganda—that many people feel strongly about. As John Lee said in *The Diplomatic Persuaders*, "One man's 'information' is another man's 'propaganda,' depending on one's point of view." But some of the confusion surrounding the subject was dispelled in a perceptive article by an unlikely author in an unlikely magazine. Gordon A. Moon, A U.S. Army information officer, wrote an article entitled "Information Officer or Propagandist?" which appeared in the December 1967 issue of *Army* magazine. He clarified two important points about the nature of propaganda. One point is that the purpose of propaganda is not only to create or change attitudes, but also to influence behavior. The other point is that there is a propaganda spectrum. At one end of the spectrum is bad or exploitive propaganda. At the other is the not so bad, utilitarian propaganda.

In support of Moon's first point, nearly everyone works in one way or another at influencing the behavior of others. This includes all types of people in roles such as parents, teachers, officers, policemen, salesmen, preachers, lawyers, politicians, and bosses, and to survive in our capitalist society a company must influence behavior by convincing people to buy its products, invest in its stock, come to work for it, or allow it to do things such as build a plant or enter a merger.

So the question naturally arises: is everyone who tries to influence behavior using propaganda? In a sense, it seems they are.

Numerous attempts have been made to determine when information is propaganda and when it is not. Ralph D. Casey, for many years director of the School of Journalism at the University of Minnesota, said that propgandists are *interested* informers, while newsmen are *disinterested* informers. There is of course a great deal of meaning in this, but it does not completely clarify the distinction. It is probably safe to say that propagandists *are* always interested informers. It is less safe to assert that editors and reporters are universally disinterested informers.

Another method of differentiating propaganda from other information was formulated by novelist William Burroughs. It is described by Tony Tanner in his book of literary criticism, *City of Words*. According to

Tanner, "Burroughs himself once worked in an advertising agency and he is aware of the necessity to differentiate the activity of the writer from that of the copy-writer. This he does by discriminating between different intentions. He is manipulating words and images, not to make people accept and purchase existing products and artifacts, but to 'create an alteration in the reader's consciousness.' "

This may work well for Burroughs, but it is not too good as a practical ethical standard for publicity specialists. Their intention is an out-and-out attempt to influence behavior, possibly even to convince people to accept and purchase things. They might even try to create an alteration in the consciousness of others to accomplish this.

The point of all this is that propaganda can be positive as well as negative; it can be constructive as well as exploitive. It is at worst a manufactured version of reality, and at best honest and complete information which serves some useful purpose. And although the distinction is sometimes exceedingly fine, it is important to try to distinguish between the positive and negative characteristics of propaganda. One approach is to look at its techniques.

Propaganda Techniques

In the following listing, the first column contains many of the propaganda techniques. All are ordinarily used in the negative application of propaganda, such as in psychological warfare. The propaganda techniques used in publicity are checked in the second column.

Propaganda Techniques	Used in Publicity
Deliberate lies	
Evasion	
Quibbling	
Double-talk	
Omission of facts	
Distortion of facts	
Exaggeration	
Simplification	X
Dogmatic statements	
Prejudice appeals	
Quoting an authority	X
Confusing statements	
Labeling	X
Name-calling	
Finding scapegoats	
Symbolism	X
Testimonials	X

Construed quotations	X
Appealing to emotions	X
Use of dramatics	X
Claims of universality	
Provocation	
Delaying tactics	
Exploiting events	X
Selected arguments	X

So it seems that Moon's second point—the idea of a propaganda spectrum—also has validity, and that there is one area of the spectrum where we find exploitative propaganda, such as that used by Hitler and Goebbels, but there is another area where well-intentioned propaganda appears.

But however one explains propaganda, it still sounds like a dirty word to most people. So to get around the mental revulsion toward the word itself, another term is needed. News management is a possibility, but it does not really describe publicity. A better term may be "engineered messages."

According to Alvin Toffler, writing in *Future Shock*, an engineered message is tight, condensed, and not redundant. "it is," he says, "highly purposeful, preprocessed to eliminate unnecessary repetition, consciously designed to maximize informational content. It is, as communications theorists say, 'information-rich.' "

In the publicity sense, engineered messages are intended to persuade and to motivate. But they must be more than just information-rich. In order to be persuasive, they must first attract attention. An added requirement is that they be believable. Another way of saying it is that the messages must be noteworthy, and they must be true.

In publicity in general, but in industrial publicity especially, the element of believability is extremely important. The audiences for industrial publicity are more often than not informed groups who will not be swayed by unfounded persuasion.

So one of the more important characteristics of publicity is that is must be true. As Abraham Lincoln said, "If you call a tail a leg, how many legs has a dog? Five? No, calling a tail a leg don't *make* it a leg."

THE MEDIA VIEWPOINT

Journalists often distrust industry and look at publicity with attitudes ranging from wary acceptance to outright contempt. They rightly see it as engineered messages, but to them such messages are suspect. Industry, along with most other types of organizations, however, feels it is entitled to use publicity to put its story across, and that engineered messages are not only desirable but necessary. It is partly because of this difference of opinion that a journalist often assumes the role of an adversary.

Journalistic Adversaries

The vast majority of industry and other executives and workers is reasonably decent and honest. But everyone tends to try to protect himself and his organization. Journalists must sometimes penetrate that protection to assure themselves and their readers that it is just protection and not the hiding of something against the public interest or maybe even corrupt or illegal.

Put another way, the role of journalistic adversary is a necessary one in our society in that it is a key element of a strong free press. Dale Minor, in *The Information War*, said: "The essential function of the press in a free society is to provide information to a free citizenry who are presumed competent to evaluate that information and make up their minds as to their best course of action or inaction, as the case may be. The very structure of and fabric of democrary is founded upon this presumption."

There are of course abuses of freedom of the press. These can only be considered one of the prices companies must pay for operating in a society that encourages a free press as well as free enterprise.

The two prominent reasons for abuses of freedom of the press are shallow reporting and sensationalism. In the first case, the journalist does not delve deeply enough into the subject, or fails to check his facts to the extent that he should. This may be due to inexperience, but it is more often due to the competitive urge to scoop everyone and put something in print as quickly as possible. In the case of sensationalism, there is an attempt to make a story more interesting than it actually is.

The role of adversary is at one extreme a negative viewpoint. A case for this viewpoint was made by Dale Minor. "Journalism must be largely negative," he said, "for the simple reason that the journalist, like the doctor, deals in pathology. And who would think of asking his doctor to concentrate on what is right with him? By the same token—by the criterion of importance to the public—hunger, oppression, riots, wars, and the conditions that breed them are properly news, whereas peace and healthy people are not." He went on to say that there *is* a place for constructive and positive coverage, but it is considerably less important and carries a much lower priority than "persistent and emergent problems that the public must understand and attempt to solve,"

As indicated above, the negative viewpoint is an extreme. It is interesting, although maybe not entirely relevant, that at the other extreme are the advocate journalists. They are mostly found on the staffs of highly specialized trade and technical publications, and actively advocate the interests of their trade or industry. But their advocacy is usually within the bounds of editorial integrity. They retain the right to criticize their trade or industry as well as support it.

So it must be recognized that industry uses engineered messages and journalists often take an adversary position. These two viewpoints can never be completely reconciled, but the negative effects can be minimized if both sides recognize they have differing viewpoints based on different goals which sometimes come into conflict.

The Adversary has Adversaries

Journalism is of course not above criticism. It has in fact come under increasing attack in the recent past, both from within and without. Accustomed to being on the offense in criticizing the believability of government and industry, journalists are being told they have a credibility gap of their own. Lester Markel's article, entitled, "Why the Public Doesn't Trust the Press," in the August 15, 1972, issue of *World Magazine* is an example of recent criticism. He said,

> The press generally likes to believe that a prime reason for the credibility gap is the tendency of the reader-listener to blame the editors for the blackness of the news. This argument has a shadow of substance to it. But only a shadow. There are more solid reasons for the mistrust of many newspapers, among them these three: inaccuracy (shoddy reporting, sensational editing, lack of perspective); irresponsibility (abandonment of objectivity, disregard of national security, disinterest in the public interest); inaccessibility (blindness to minority viewpoints, identification with the Establishment roster and dogma).

Media Dependence on Press Relations

No large-scale studies have been made that show how dependent the media actually is on public relations in general or industrial publicity specifically. But most interested observers feel that the dependency is substantial. Here are some typical quotes.

From Burt Zollo's *The Dollars and Cents of Public Relations*:

> Prof. Ralph Ober of New York's New School for Social Research estimated that 80 percent of all newspaper stories come from PR.

> Chicago's *American* editor Ernest Tucker: "It would be impossible for us to cover all the things we are supposed to cover, or even to find out about, without

the able assistance of PR people. We understand perfectly and fully the important part—the indispensible part—the PR fraternity plays in putting out daily newspapers.

Nicholas R. Shuman, an assistant managing editor of the Chicago *Daily News*, made the same point when he said, "The bald truth is that he who puts out the financial section of a daily newspaper could not do his job without the press relations people. Most of the news in business and finance must originate with PR. This still might be a revelation to a few old testament city editors."

From an article by Harry S. Ashmore entitled "Government by Public Relations," in the September/October 1971 issue of *The Center Magazine*:

The media as presently constituted could not function without the array of skills and resources provided them without cost in the name of public relations.

CONCLUSIONS ON NEWS MANAGEMENT

In the final analysis, it must be said that industrial publicity does use some form of news management. But such management has very severe limitations. This was brought into focus in an *Aviation Week & Space Technology* editorial by the magazine's editor, Robert B. Hotz. He said, "In a society with a free press it is difficult to suppress the facts for long, and it is impossible to manage the news very effectively to maintain the desired image for long if the facts do not support it."

This statement reflects the delicate balance of company objectives and editorial needs and requirements that must be maintained for industrial publicity to be of value to anyone. It points up the fact that truth is the ultimate criterion for the usefulness of publicity. If the facts do not support what an organization is publicly saying about itself, the organization will sooner or later be found out. Once this happens, it will be a long time before that organization is completely trusted again.

Even if an organization uses news management in one form or another, it must never attempt to manage journalists. That is, it should never attempt to "use" the press in the exploitative sense of the word. Such efforts are usually doomed to failure, and give an organization a very noticeable black eye.

On Total News Management

Total news management, which is total control over the editorial coverage devoted to an organization, is simply not possible in this country, if anywhere. So the only part of news that can be managed is what an organization says about itself to the world; in a word, its publicity. But questions from journalists are different. They should be answered as quickly and truthfully as possible. To do otherwise is not only improper, but is also dangerous.

On Professionalism

The special skills of professionals are usually needed to do the publicity job. Or they should at least be used to point the way. They have two important characteristics—sensitivity to public attitudes and ability to communicate with the public—that for many executives are not well developed.

Another reason professional skills or advice are important is that journalists and businessmen have different ways of looking at the world. A publicity professional has the skill to interpret one for the other.

In Summary

To summarize much of what this chapter has tried to say, the following is what a major corporation's public relations vice-president told a meeting of some of the company's executives:

> We cannot hide for long major actions by the corporation, such as large acquisitions, plant shutdowns, major cutbacks in the work force, strikes, new plants or significant expansions, serious accidents, or key operational changes. Recognizing this, we have a policy to communicate to our audiences, as freely and as frankly as possible. We do not say "no comment" to the press. If we cannot release information, we say so, and try to explain why. And it is necessary to withhold information, at times, when final decisions have not been made, or when future release dates have been established for sound reasons.
> We can gain respect for ourselves by the way we communicate, by building a reputation for honesty and integrity and fairness, by being responsive to the needs of the press and of the community, and of people everywhere.

REFERENCES

Harry S. Ashmore, "Government by Public Relations," *The Center Magazine*, September/ October 1971, Vol. IV, No. 5.

Rex F. Harlow, Social Science in Public Relations, "Harper and Brothers, New York, 1957.

Robert B. Hotz, Editorial, *Aviation Week & Space Technology*, March 18, 1963.

Jon Lee, Ed., *The Diplomatic Persuaders*, John Wiley & Sons, Inc., New York, 1968.

Lester Markel, "Why the Public Doesn't Trust the Press," *World Magazine*, August 15, 1972, Vol. 1, No. 4.

Dale Minor, *The Information War*, Hawthorne Books, New York, 1970.

Gordon A. Moon, "Information Officer or Propagandist?" *Army*, December 1967.

Clarence B. Randall, *The Folklore of Management*, New American Library, New York, 1961.

Alvin Toffler, *Future Shock*, Random House, Inc., New York, 1970.

Tony Tanner, *City of Words*, Harper & Row, New York, 1971.

Burt Zollo, *The Dollars and Cents of Public Relations*, McGraw Hill Book Company, New York, 1967.

3
THE APPLICATION OF
INDUSTRIAL PUBLICITY

FUNDAMENTALS OF APPLYING PUBLICITY

The Publicity Process

The diagram in Figure 3-1 shows how the objective feeds to the message, the message to the medium, and the medium to the audience. But before the process can be really effective, the relationships between the elements of the process must be determined. Certain relationships and elements can be fine-tuned to achieve the best possible operation of the total process.

As the illustration also indicates, characteristics of the audience are reflected back to and influence the medium, the message, and the objective. The medium in turn influences the message and the objective. The message does not influence the objective in any significant way, so there is no feedback arrow from message to objective. This is because the message is the tool in the process. It is nothing until it is formulated by an objective and modified to take into account the other elements in the network. The elements in the figure are interrelated. A change in one may mean changes in the others. This is the main reason for feedback.

Audience

Without an audience, there is no need for a medium. And without a medium, the message has nowhere to go. Without an audience and a medium, consequently, the objective is meaningless.

The subject of audience keeps coming up because it is a pivotal consideration. This means that the first rule of good publicity is that it must be tailored for the specific audiences it is intended to reach. If it is, it is probably considered noteworthy by the audiences, which means that it is probably considered newsworthy by the media that serve them.

Audiences can probably be broken down into two categories. The first is

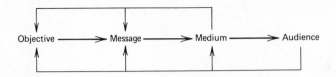

Figure 3-1.   Publicity process flow diagram.

the general public, and the second is specialized publics. The general public includes all the specialized publics.

The term "general public" is way up on the scale of abstraction. What it includes depends on who defines it. But it usually means everyone who reads newspapers and general-interest magazines like newsweeklies, and who watches television and listens to radio.

Specialized publics are segments, usually readily definable, of the general public. The following is a listing that might be typical for a company.

Customers	A community
Employees	Distributors (retailers, wholesalers, manufacturers' agents)
Investors	Suppliers
Financial analysts	Members of an industry (steel, mining, electronics)
Bankers	Special-interest groups (e.g., environmentalists)
Legislators	
Regulatory agencies	
Local governments	

The nature of the audience determines the nature of the media that serve them. An example of the way this works is shown in Figure 3-2. Although the lists of audiences and publications differ to some degree from one company to another, the matrix in the figure is fairly typical.

Goals and Objectives

In a company, publicity must be instrumental in achieving company goals. If it is not, any responsible executive will not allow time and money to be spent on it. But there are many uses of publicity that do foster company goals. Some of these goals are:

• Increasing the share of the market.
• Entering new markets.
• Improving recognition.
• Influencing legislation.
• Encouraging outside investment in the company.

	Customers	Employees	Investors	Financial Analysts	Bankers	Legislators	Regulatory Agencies	Local Governments	Community	Distributors and Suppliers
Association journals	X									
Professional magazines	X		X	X	X		X			
Industrial magazines	X		X	X	X					X
Trade and merchandising magazines	X		X	X	X					X
Business magazines and papers	X		X	X	X	X	X			X
Newspapers	X	X	X	X	X	X	X	X	X	
Electronic media	X	X	X	X	X	X	X	X	X	
Company publications	X	X	X	X	X	X	X	X	X	X

Figure 3-2 Media-audience matrix.

- Attracting diversification prospects.
- Stimulating acquisition.
- Pacifying stockholders.
- Keeping the company's community happy.
- Stimulating industry action.
- Influencing legislation.
- Going public.

These goals naturally fall into two categories of company functions. The first four in the list have, or could have, a relationship to the marketing domain. The rest are largely in the bailiwick of general management. So it appears publicity serves two masters, marketing and general management. In some companies, marketing publicity usually comes under the heading of product publicity or technical publicity. In most companies general management publicity comes under public relations.

PUBLIC RELATIONS PUBLICITY

Nature of Public Relations

Much has been written about the nature and purpose of public relations, so the intent here is not to explore these in any great depth.

One way to look at public relations is to compare the definitions offered by some experts. Edward L. Bernays, a public relations pioneer, suggested a simple definition in *Perspective in Public Relations.* "Public Relations," he said, "is good works understood by the public." But this may be too simple to reveal any insight.

Paul Burton, in *Corporate Public Relations,* proposed that "public relations is a function of management which helps a company establish and maintain a good name for itself and its products and services through professional communications techniques."

Kershon Kekst, vice-president, Ruder & Finn, Inc., writing in *Public Utilities Fortnightly* magazine, gave as his definition: "Public relations can be defined as a management function which evaluates public attitudes, identifies the policies and procedures of an organization with public interest, and executes a program of action and communication to earn public understanding and acceptance."

In a session devoted to public relations at the American Mining Congress Convention in Denver, September 1967, Gerald K. Skibbons, vice-president, Opinion Research Corporation, presented a formula. He said that $x + y = $ PR. The first letter in the equation, x, stands for what an organization does and how well it performs. The y stands for how well and how often the organization explains itself to others.

For some observers, none of the definitions ring completely true. They agree with what Ivy Lee, considered the founder of modern public relations, once said about his work, "I have never been able to find a satisfactory phrase to describe what I do."

However public relations is defined, it is not synonymous with publicity. One way of looking at it is that public relations develops messages; publicity delivers them to the right place, at the right time in the right way. This illustrates that publicity is a tool used to fulfill public relations objectives. But many public relations agencies and many company public relations departments are little more than publicity mills which crank out press releases. Such publicity suffers from lack of purpose and relevancy. But when publicity is properly planned and executed, it has a positive effect on the image, stature, reputation, and recognition of a company. The importance of this is exemplified by the fact that the good name of a company has a cash value. A good name takes years, sometimes even decades, to develop.

Although publicity designed to accomplish public relations objectives has an effect on profitability, the relationship is hard to describe, especially in terms of orders entered. The relationship is clearer, but still not always completely tangible, between sales and publicity designed to meet marketing objectives.

Publicity for Image Building

The subject of the company image was covered to an extent in Chapter 1. It was pointed out that, if individuals know and respect a company, it is assumed they will be inclined to buy its products or services and allow it to do certain things. This is true of all companies, no matter what type or size. At one extreme might be a large multinational, multiproduct corporation. This type of company has many publics and many images. At the other extreme might be a very small company which is highly specialized. It might have but one important image, that of, say, the company's distributors. The more deserving of respect a company is, the more distributors will be attracted, and they will be inclined to perform better for a company they know and like.

Image publicity that could help the small company's cause might be news about its excellent delivery and service record, both of which distributors value highly. It might be information about the smooth-working cooperative advertising plan of the company. Another example might be news of a communications system installed by the company to make it able to respond better and faster to distributor questions. A different approach would be for the company to obtain and have published case histories about the use of its products, material that prominently mentions the distributors as well as the company.

Financial Publicity

Next to customers, the most important public or audience of a publicly owned company is the investors who buy stock. This audience is not as important to a privately owned company, but that does not mean it can be ignored. For one thing, the company will probably want to go public sometime in the future. For another, the financial community is the pipeline for capital.

Communicating to the financial community is complicated by the fact that a company has thousands of competitors in the stock market, which are vying for attention. This is in contrast to the limited number of other firms competing for a company's product sales.

The world of finances is so specialized that it seems arcane to outsiders. So it is necessary that financial publicity be directed by financial public relations counselors or by financial executives with a strong sensitivity to public attitudes and reactions.

Financial publicity falls into two categories. The first is aimed at the financial community. The other is image-building publicity which is more general in nature. The first is highly specific information which is mainly intended to inform the members of the financial community about a company's financial status. For example, earnings reports are probably the most common form of financial press releases. Image-building publicity may be financial in nature, but usually is about other aspects of a company's affairs. It is designed to tell stockholders and the financial community about the whole range of a company's progress, abilities, and intentions.

Not all stockholders are members of the financial community. There has been a large upsurge in "grass roots" investing in stock. Among grass roots investors are employees enrolled in fringe benefit stock purchase plans, members of investment clubs, and individuals who play the stock market as a sideline or hobby. The financial community consists of security analysts, brokers, investment counselors, underwriters, mutual fund, bank, and trust investment officers, and financial editors.

The financial community is reached primarily through a relatively small number of professional and specialized publications in the field. Grass roots stockholders *and* the financial community are reached through the same media used for general public relations image building.

Studies have shown that a company's image definitely influences price-earnings ratios, prices of shares, and availability of financing. This is borne out by the tremendous effect catstrophic bad news about a company, such as a major antitrust case, can have on a company's stock.

Members of the financial community rely on much more than financial facts and figures directed at them. These are history which does not always tell how a company will perform in the future. So it is necessary to communicate to them somehow the future aims of the company and its ability to carry them out.

In general, the objective of financial publicity is to maintain and improve the company's image. The company must appear innovative and forward-looking. It must try to broaden general public and financial community recognition and good will.

Some more specific objectives of financial publicity are:

- Attract new investors.
- Maintain existing investors' loyalty.
- Build investor confidence to assure that they use their proxies in a favorable way.
- Help maintain stock stability, a factor considered very important by analysts and brokers.
- Pave the way for added financing.
- Prepare for a merger or acquisition.
- Stimulate the interest of top executive and technical talent.
- Maintain or improve relations with regulatory agencies, tax authorities, and other government bodies that impinge on the financial area.
- Encourage stockholders to buy the company's products.

There is an important limitation on the use of financial publicity: Security and Exchange Commission (SEC) regulations. These make it unlawful to promote the sale of stock any time after a registration statement has been filed with the SEC and before it becomes effective. In a set of guidelines (Release No. 5180) the SEC says:

The publication of information and statements, and publicity efforts, made in advance of a proposed offering which have the effect of conditioning the public mind or arousing public interest in the issuer or in its securities constitutes an offer (to sell) in violation of the Act. The same holds true with respect to publication of information which is part of the selling effort between the filing date and the effective date of a registration statement.

Further on, the guidelines state:

Issuers and their representatives should not initiate publicity when in registration, but should nevertheless respond to legitimate inquiries for factual information about the company's financial condition and business operations. Further, care should be exercised so that, for example, predictions, projections, forecasts, estimates and opinions concerning value are not given with respect to such things, among others, as sales and earnings and value of the issuer's securities.

MARKETING PUBLICITY

A Sales Tool

An industrial executive was quoted in *Business Week* as saying, "Our public image is important, but first we have to make sure that we stay in business." And for a company to stay in business, it must consistently sell its products or services and make money in the bargain. Publicity is widely used to help this process in a more direct way than image building. This type of publicity can be called marketing publicity.

The practice of publicity as a marketing tool draws on public relations for some of its techniques. But it also requires an understanding of products and service features, the selling process, and the nature of customers. This understanding is in the domain of the marketing function.

In some companies, marketing publicity comes under the banner of public relations. In others, it is under marketing where it may go by titles such as product publicity or technical publicity. Since some small companies have marketing but no public relations department, marketing publicity of course is done by the marketing department.

It is probably safe to say that industry puts a lot more of its resources into marketing publicity than into public relations publicity. This may very well be appropriate for most companies, depending on the type of business the company is in and on the company's situation. However, companies tend to ignore the need for public relations publicity until they have a severe problem on their hands. So, at some point in a company's life, it needs to establish a public relations function, and it is better if it is sooner rather than later.

One of the ways in which publicity is useful in marketing is to help meet competition. In many lines of business, competition is so keen that it is hard to maintain a marketing advantage for any length of time. This especially applies to such factors as price, distribution, or point-of-sale promotional aids. But publicity properly used can produce a competitive edge, especially in lines of business in which the competition does not have a good understanding of it. For example, some segments of industry, such as electronic component manufacturing, are largely made up of small companies which may lack publicity know-how. They are just trying to stay in business. (This can also apply to a division or subsidiary of a big corporation. These are often semiautonomous and get little attention from the corporate publicity specialists who are involved in things on the corporate level that are perhaps more important and perhaps more interesting.)

Other reasons for the usefulness of publicity are the problems and cost of direct selling, when a salesman has to call on someone. It has been estimated that personal selling reaches only one in six of the people who influence the buying of a product or service. Publicity, along with advertising and direct mail, can be used to reach the five buying influences the salesman cannot.

Another factor is expense. The cost of the average sales call by a salesman has been variously pegged at $19.06, $28.04, $31.31, and $35.55 for different types of salesmen in different fields. Anything that can help sell indirectly helps reduce the cost of selling. Publicity can in certain cases do this.

Product Publicity

The role publicity plays in marketing is most often in the area of product publicity. (The term product is used here to mean not only a physical item, hardware, but also software or services.) This is publicity about something for sale. Some insight into how it works may be gained from a case described by John F. Budd, Jr., in *An Executive Primer on Public Relations.* The case concerns Bulova's introduction of its Accutron watch. The company's feeling was that it had made a technical breakthrough and needed an intensive educational campaign. Three separate types of journalists were identified. The first were shopping column editors of monthly home, service, and women's publications; the second were editors of technical publications, and the third were general press writers.

Three separate press briefings tailored to their editorial audiences were held at different times to take into account the lead times of the three groups. The shopping column editors were briefed and given material 3 months before the actual public introduction of the watch. The technical editors were briefed a month in advance of the public event. Although secrecy was emphasized, these groups of editors knew that they were being told in advance for their own benefit. They reciprocated by not using or leaking the story in advance.

The public unveiling was at a press conference held before a group of 200 general press journalists in New York City. Separate simultaneous press conferences had been arranged in 13 other cities, which were connected to the main event in New York by closed-circuit television.

Major media in 32 market areas scheduled for advertising were contacted by the company. Also, media in key cities not included in the telecast press conference were contacted. In both cases, information and photos were made available. A total of 272 editors in 62 cities was contacted.

A great amount of interest was stimulated by Bulova's intensive publicity program. The success of the Accutron line was in part a result of it, because the editorial coverage had presold customers. This preconditioning subsequently was reinforced by an intensive advertising campaign and continued publicity.

Examples of product and service publicity press releases appear in Chapter 9. Both Chapter 8 and 9 go into some detail about the nature and handling of such releases.

In addition to the very important job of informing people about things to buy, product publicity can also serve in what can be called a market research and development role. One such area is market identification.

Once a product is ready to be put on the market, the marketing department may not be able to identify and locate the customers precisely. Also, they may know some applications of a product but not all. In some cases, publicity can be used both to help identify the customers and to find out about new applications.

An example of how this works was given by George Hammond of Carl Byoir & Associates in a talk:

> A few years ago, Honeywell's research scientists developed an ultra-violet tube that could detect flame, smoke and odor simultaneously. The company knew the tube would be valuable in improving flame safeguard equipment, and it was. But there was a general feeling among engineers and marketing people alike that it offered potential for many other, if the possible applications could only be found.
>
> So to help, we did an extensive publicity job on the new tube. A total of 1600 inquiries resulted. From these the marketing people compiled a list of fifty possible applications they had not previously known about, and some of these have since been successfully developed.

Yet another use of marketing publicity is to have information published about professional firms. Examples of such organizations are consulting engineering, architectural, and urban planning firms. In most cases, it is professionally unethical for such organizations to advertise, and publicity can to an extent be used as a substitute. Such publicity takes the form of newsworthy examples of services the firm has performed, which find their way into magazines and newspapers.

Both press releases and signed articles can be used for this type of publicity. Press releases can be aimed at newspapers, specialized publications, or both. Signed articles are written for specialized publications. For example, a consulting engineer involved in the mechanical equipment part of the design of a new shopping center might write an article about how he solved a special problem. The article might then be submitted to a publication that reaches heating, air conditioning, and plumbing businesses.

Once information about a company's products or services is published, it can be used additionally as a marketing tool. Articles can be reprinted inexpensively and used for direct mail and as a handout for salesmen to leave with customers. It is conceivable that the reprint might be the reason for having the information published in the first place. This may occur when it is necessary to contact a very large number of customers with a third-party endorsement. The fact that an editor is willing to use the information amounts to a kind of endorsement, and people find editorial material far more believable than advertising material or sales literature.

Reprinting is a valuable tool, but there is a major caution that should be observed. It is illegal to reprint copyrighted material without the copyright owner's consent, and publications are almost without exception copyrighted. So before reprinting an article, the publisher must be contacted and his permission obtained. Most publishers want such requests in writing. If there is some urgency, a publisher may accept a teletype in lieu of a letter. Or he may give a go-ahead over the telephone if he is assured that a letter will be written as a post facto request for permission.

Some publications are reluctant to give permission for reprinting because they like to reprint articles themselves to make a small profit and to insure quality reprints. In these cases, the publishers will usually agree to print the company's name or logotype on the back of the reprint.

REFERENCES

Edward L. Bernays, *Public Relations*, University of Oklahoma Press, Norman, Okla., 1963.

John F. Budd, Jr., *An Executive's Primer on Public Relations*, Chilton Book Company, Philadelphia, Pa., 1969.

Paul Burton, *Corporate Public Relations*, Reinhold Publishing Corporation, New York, N.Y., 1966.

George Hammond, "Remarks," Association of Industrial Advertisers 42nd Annual Conference, Philadelphia, Pa., July 1, 1964.

Kenneth Henry, "Perspective on Public Relations," *Harvard Business Review*, July–August, 1967.

Kershon Kekst, "Special Audience Communication: Public Relations Cornerstone," *Public Utilities Fortnightly*, June 10, 1965, Vol. 75, No. 12.

David Skylar, "A Quiet Revolution. . .the Rise of the Corporate Image," *Industrial Marketing*, September 1967.

Burt Zollo, *The Dollars and Sense of Public Relations*, McGraw-Hill Book Company, New York, N.Y., 1967.

4

THE TOTAL INDUSTRIAL
COMMUNICATIONS
APPROACH

Industrial publicity is but one tool in the arsenal of what might be called industrial communications. Some of the other tools are advertising, sales literature, exhibits, and company publications. Using the tools together in a properly planned program is the most effective and sensible approach in telling a company's story. But in many cases, companies either do not utilize all the tools available to them, or fail to use them in an effective and coordinated way.

THE CONCEPT OF TOTAL COMMUNICATIONS

Total or integrated communications is a subject too broad in scope to be treated in any great detail here, but it is too important to ignore. The following treatment is necessarily cursory.

All business transactions involve one form of communications or another. The results of these transactions in most cases depend on how well the people involved understand each other. So it is necessary to use the best combination of tools and to use them with exactness to assure that communication does occur.

The total communications approach is oriented toward problems and programs. Communications tools are oriented toward tasks. In using the total approach, problems are defined and then broken into their elements or subproblems, and the tools of communications are then brought to bear on these elements or subproblems. For example, the Accutron watch campaign cited in Chapter 3 used all the tools of communications in attacking the problem of telling watch buyers about the breakthrough and presenting the advantages of the product in a way that would provide the greatest impact. Bulova used every communications tool—including publicity, direct mail, advertising, sales literature, point-of-sale promotion—to its utmost in the right places and at the right times.

All the tools should play a role in an effective communications program. But different problems mean different mixtures and different weightings of the tools. Budgets also have a large influence on what tools are used and when they are used. Small companies often simply cannot afford large campaigns like the Accutron promotion. So they tend to emphasize lower-cost tools such as publicity and direct mail, and often veto space advertising on the basis of cost. And to an extent, some of the tools can be used in place of each other. But it must be remembered that the tools are complementary, and any attempt to completely substitute one for another is probably doomed to at least partial failure.

Total Communications Approach

Figure 4-1 shows an approach to total communications that is fairly typical in industry. It defines the messages to be communicated to the audiences that are important to the profitability—and sometimes the survival—of the company. It also shows the diversity of communications tools used to convey messages. Some of the tools, such as the annual report, have limited usefulness; others, such as advertising and publicity, have more uses.

It is important to note that the messages are not defined in a vacuum. They are established within the dual framework of the company's short- and long-range goals and the attitudes of the company's various publics.

Another important observation is that communications is not the only major influence on sales, profitability, and reputation. Many other forces and pressures are at work; they vary in importance from one company to the next. Some of the other influences are salesmen; product price, quality, availability, and features; plant location, convenience, and labor situation; inventory policies and distribution methods; service policies, availability and quality.

Necessity for the Total Approach

Everyone probably agrees that, like motherhood, the concept of total communications is good. But it really is a lot of trouble. It takes a great deal of planning, coordination, missionary work, and follow-up. These things take time, something always in short supply in industry. So the question naturally arises, "Is it worth the trouble?" The answer is, "Usually."

One of the most telling arguments favoring a total communications approach is that this method has cost and effectiveness advantages. As a general rule, if different tasks with a lot in common are carried out

Our Story	How We Tell Our Story	To Our Publics
The company:		
Produces quality products and services	Newspaper, magazine, television, and radio advertising and editorial coverage. Speeches, booklets, and special projects	General public
Is a good company with which to do business	Business and financial press advertising and editorial coverage. Annual report, security analysts mailings, and meetings	Business and financial community
Is a valuable asset to the nation's industrial, social, and economic life, and a "good citizen" in the communities in which it operates	Annual report, annual meeting, stockholder newsletter, letters, and special reports	Stockholders
	Letters, special mailings, personal contacts, speech reprints, government committee testimony, and newspaper and magazine advertising and editorial coverage	Government
Is a pioneer in research, engineering, and product development	Trade and technical magazines, newspapers, and general magazine advertising and editorial coverage. Company magazine, annual report, speeches, article reprints, and special mailings	Customers
Is a fair employer of competent, highly skilled people	Technical magazines, speeches and papers, company magazine, and newspapers	Engineers, scientists, educators
Is a well-managed company serving the best interest of customers, owners, employees, and the public	Company newspaper, letters, workplace meetings, supervisor meetings, booklets, bulletin boards, family days, films, annual report, and in-plant displays	Employees
	Newspaper advertising and editorial coverage, television and radio, open houses, speeches and their reprints, films, community projects, and community participation in decisions affecting it	Plant or office communities

Figure 4-1 Typical industrial communications approach.

independently, there is likely to be redundancy and there very likely will be conflict due to the different groups getting in each other's way or crossing each other's lines. This kind of situation is antisynergistic, and produces results that are less than adequate for costs that are higher than they need to be.

Another compelling reason for using a total approach is that many problems companies face are not single-function problems. That is, such problems are not exclusively sales, distribution, service, technological reputation, financial standing, or community relations problems. They are usually combination problems. They must be attacked on a unified basis. Individual departments—such as marketing, engineering, or industrial relations—cannot effectively mount their own efforts toward solving problems wider in scope than the department's.

Yet another argument pointing up the need for total communications is one that is tied strongly to human nature and its consequences in an organization. When communications groups and people in different specialties, such as advertising and publicity, are not persuaded to work together either by circumstances or by policy, they often compete. For example, when advertising and public relations personnel report to entirely different segments of a company, and when there is not strong communications direction from top management, the advertising and public relations managers may actively compete. One of the main reasons for this is that they are trying to achieve similar results through different means. And each may feel his way is better or more effective. Advertising and public relations managers might compete for funds; they very probably would compete for those fundamental ingredients of power and influence, points.

Although there may be many other good reasons in favor of a total communications approach, it may suffice for the moment to give this final reason: A good communications program can be a competitive edge. For example, a competing company might have a communications program that is strong in publicity but weak in advertising. Another competitor might have the reverse. A third might be weak in both. If a company is strong in the use of all the communications tools, it will very likely have a strong competitive advantage.

In view of all these important reasons supporting the concept of total communications, it is legitimate to ask why it is not universally used. The answer is that there are in most companies a variety of forces and pressures which make it difficult to achieve a comprehensive program with unified direction.

One reason is the dependence on direct selling. Good sales managers who have come up through the sales ranks tend to favor face-to-face selling over indirect methods such as those used in communications. Such individuals tend to downgrade the usefulness of the communications in the selling of products and services.

Another reason is the intangible nature of communications. Because its results are difficult to measure, it does not receive the same attention as day-to-day activities in which the results are highly visible—such as the shipment of a product on which delivery is overdue.

Sometimes these tendencies—reliance on direct selling and the suspect nature of communications because it defies easy analysis—are found in the same individual. This can occur in the case of an executive who has worked as a sales engineer in a highly technical field.

Yet another reason why total communications is not as widely practiced as it might be is that the individuals in companies who are responsible for communications usually have come up to their job from a specialized subdiscipline, such as advertising. Because of the intangible nature of their work, they can and often do skew their activity toward what they are most interested in, or toward what is fashionable at the time in the company. This can have some important consequences. One is that the total communications job is not done. The other is that some other person or group in a different functional area may gradually move in and begin to do the part of the job that has been defaulted. This, of course, results in fragmentation, diffusion of authority, and a lack of central direction.

There is yet another reason why the total communications approach is absent in some companies. This reason, which was alluded to earlier, is the complete separation of public relations and advertising in some companies. Some observers feel this seriously limits the effectiveness of communications; others feel there are good reasons for the two to be separate. For example, a case can be made for the assertion that, when public relations is dominated by advertising, it tends to lose its objectivity.

Public relations and advertising grew up in industry in response to different forces and in separate functional parts of companies. The industrial revolution spawned advertising as a marketing technique for conveying information about products to customers. Public relations, as mentioned in Chapter 1, was developed by industry management to help rid itself of the bad image it had acquired as a result of the excesses of some of the mighty industrialists, and to teach the industrialists how to modify their attitudes and methods to make their ways of doing business more acceptable to the public.

So advertising and public relations were developed to serve different needs. But they since have been forced closer together by the changing requirements of society and new ways of doing business.

There are at least two points of convergence of modern advertising and public relations. One is at the point of image building. Both the publicity tools of public relations and the tools of advertising are used in the building, or maintaining, of a company's image, whether with a small, specialized public or several more general publics. The other point of convergence is where the publicity tools of public relations are used in concert with advertising tools to help sell products and services.

But because of the historical separation of public relations and advertising in many established companies, the two do not work together as well as they might. Where this situation exists, top management direction is needed to assure an effective communications program.

A recognition of the need to bring public relations and advertising closer together is cited by John F. Budd, Jr., in *An Executive's Primer on Public Relations*. He points out that smaller companies that are just getting around to setting up a communications organization, or even some larger companies that are just beginning to formalize their public relations activities, tend to incorporate both public relations and advertising in one job. In most instances, Budd continues, the companies tend to "give the public relations director responsibility for advertising as well."

Budd also refers to a widely quoted statement that seems to sum it up. The statement is attributed to Whit Hobbs, senior vice-president of Benton & Bowles. He said, "Public relations and advertising may not be legally married, but they sure as hell have an arrangement."

Organizing to Do the Total Job

There is probably no ideal way to organize for the total communications job. Companies differ widely in their structure, their markets or mixture of markets, their plant and office locations and conditions, and the audiences to which they must deliver their messages. But there are some characteristics that are common to most companies.

One such characteristic is that whoever directs the communications activity must be part of the top management team. He, or they, must be kept informed on a day-to-day basis about decisions being made and courses of action being considered. He, or they, must also be given the opportunity to offer an opinion on the effect decisions and actions may have on the attitudes of general and specific audiences of the company.

Another characteristic of an effective communications organization is that it has resources adequate to do the job it is charged with. There is often a minimum level of activity necessary for a company. If the resources are not available to reach that minimum, whatever energy and money are expended may be largely wasted.

Yet another characteristic is a professional staff. Communications should be handled by experienced and professionally qualified individuals. Home-made efforts seldom achieve respectable effectiveness. And the larger a company is, the more diversified it is; and the higher the technological level of its work, the more critical the need for professional people becomes.

In some companies, a minority, all communications functions report to a single director who is part of the company's top management team. Others have central direction of communications with functionally different parts of the company executing programs. Some companies have a cooperative arrangement in which the different parts of the company concerned with communications, such as advertising and public relations, work together to plan and execute programs. The last type of setup is one in which the different parts more or less go their own way and carry out what are in extreme cases completely independent programs.

The last-mentioned type of organization is of course much less desirable. But there are quite a number of companies that use this approach and, oddly enough, for some it seems to work.

The Two Faces of Industrial Communications

The two-role idea presented in Chapter 3 for the uses of publicity can also be applied to the more general subject of industrial communications. One of the roles discussed was support for marketing objectives; the other was support for general management or public relations objectives.

Marketing support communications, like marketing support publicity, is aimed at buyers and potential buyers of a company's products or services. Such buyers are parts of groups that are usually easy to identify. Buyer groups can nearly always be reached by using publicity or advertising through specialized publications aimed at these groups. There is a publication that reaches the boating enthusiast in the market for a new outboard motor, one that is read by the engineer who specifies electronic components for machine tool controls, and one that is published especially for purchasers of equipment for the federal government.

Communications should be as much a part of the business plan as engineering, manufacturing, or marketing. In the case in which a product is being taken to market, a communications program should be initiated no later than the time funds are committed for preproduction development. When a bidding opportunity for a service or system development contract is apparent, the communications program aimed at helping to win the contract should be in full swing well before requests for proposals are issued by whoever will fund the contract. Such a contract might be for an industrial plant process line, an automated health testing facility, or a military weapons systems.

Supporting general management or public relations objectives is the application of industrial communications tools and techniques to the building or maintenance of a company's stature or reputation—what is usually referred to by that overused and abused but still useful word *image*. Here, there is an attempt to instill or change attitudes about a company, or other organization, which is not necessarily related to its products or services.

INDUSTRIAL COMMUNICATIONS TOOLS

It is possible to divide—although somewhat arbitrarily—the tools and techniques of industrial communications into the two broad categories of publicity, advertising and sales promotion. Because of the huge amounts of money spent every year on advertising, and because of the dependence of the media—newspapers, magazines, television, and radio—on advertising revenue, advertising is the most important communications tool in financial terms. However, a surprisingly large amount of the editorial material used by the media originates as publicity. This is especially true at the specialized publications end of the communications spectrum, but less at the other end of the spectrum where the most general medium—television—appears.

Publicity

Since the subject of this book is publicity, its role as a communications tool is interwoven throughout. Later chapters deal with various aspects of publicity and its use. For example, part of Chapter 10 discusses the use of communications tools in concert. So it would be redundant to go into any detail here.

Advertising and Sales Promotion

One way of splitting up advertising and sales promotion is the following breakdown.

- Product advertising.
- Institutional advertising.
- Sales literature and aids.
- Exhibits.
- Company publications.

The term product advertising is self-explanatory. It is simply commercial messages about products (services can be products in the broad sense) which appear in space or time purchased by the advertiser. Product advertising is designed to help sell—a marketing support role.

Institutional advertising fulfills another role. It supports general management or public relations objectives. It is designed to help maintain or build the stature or reputation of a company. In most cases only large corporations can afford and justify institutional advertising. But it is also usually only large corporations that need it. Since most big companies are diversified, they must try to achieve a corporate identity that applies across the range of interests of their component parts. Smaller companies usually have a small number of products or product lines, and obtain their identity mainly from communications associated with their products.

But there is a feature of product advertising that is sometimes overlooked, namely, its effect on a company's image. For example, a manufacturer of pesticides must handle his advertising carefully these days because everyone is becoming more conscious of ecology. And no one in his right mind would have advertised napalm in the closing days of the Vietnam conflict. A true-to-life example is the communications network that the Office of Civil Defense has been developing for some time. At first, the network will have emergency radio stations in strategic locations and receivers in major police stations and other official locations. Another step, which may or may not be taken, would be to place a receiver in every home. This receiver could be activated from a transmitting station during an emergency. It is probably a good idea, but it raises the specter of a 1984 type of governmental invasion of the home. Some people are afraid that the emergency receiver could be transformed into a listening device and that private conversations would be monitored. So it is obvious that any manufacturer who wants to advertise his receivers as candidates for the network has to exercise some care in doing so. Otherwise, the company might become known as the one that is helping to bring on the era of Big Brother.

One of the main advantages of advertising over publicity is that the advertiser can say exactly what he wants to—as long as it is in good taste—because he has bought the space. Publicity must earn the space by being newsworthy. If the intneded message of the publicity does not exactly coincide with what makes it newsworthy, the message cannot be as direct as an advertising message.

Another advantage of advertising is that it can be repeated. Publicity almost always has limited usage, often just a single time.

Yet another advantage is that advertising can be exactly timed. The time publicity is used as editorial material depends to a large extent upon editors and newsmen.

But advertising is not the perfect tool; it too has limitations. The major one is that advertising has less credibility than editorial material. The editorial side of publications and electronic media is the turf of publicity. Editorial information is considered more believable than advertising, because it has been "sanctioned" by an editor through his use of it.

A major problem that continues to plague advertising men is the difficulty of measuring results. However, it is not unique to advertising; publicity also has it. At the product advertising end of the spectrum, results can usually be measured satisfactorily. Toward the other end of the spectrum, where image-building advertising is found, it is much more difficult to measure results in a meaningful way.

The category of sales literature and aids as used here includes printed material such as product information booklets and data sheets, catalogs and price lists, and application data and manuals. It also includes presentation material such as slide shows, films, flip charts, and sales pitch books. Finally, it includes direct mail material such as printed or machine-typed letters, promotional foldouts, reply cards, and samples.

The first two types of sales literature and aids mentioned are designed primarily to help salesmen sell. Sales literature, publicity, and advertising can be used effectively in conjunction with each other. But timing is important. Sales literature should be ready when the publicity begins to result in editorial coverage. If there is no publicity but space advertising is used, the literature should be available before the ads appear. If both publicity and advertising are used, the publicity should precede the advertising by enough time to allow the information to appear as editorial coverage. The reason sales literature has to be ready in advance is that editorial coverage and advertising draw inquiries from readers. These must be followed up either by sending additional information—this is where sales literature comes in—or by a salesman's call.

Reprints of favorable editorial coverage are an excellent way of combining publicity results and the idea of sales literature. Such reprints can be supplied to salesmen or used for direct mail. They have an element of believability that sales literature and advertising do not have—for the same reason given above as a disadvantage of advertising.

Direct mail material can either be in support of selling by salesmen—by uncovering prospects—or it can be used as a direct marketing tool by itself. In an article in the February 12, 1973, issue of *Advertising Age,* a tabloid trade weekly, Bob Stone described the use of direct mail in selling an electronic calculator developed by Hewlett-Packard. The product had a very good potential, but did not fit in with the company's traditional product line—sophisticated, complex, and expensive electronic equipment—which was sold by a relatively small, very proficient, highly trained force of sales engineers. So the company developed a direct mail program to sell the calculator to engineers and scientists, usually without the intervention of a Hewlett-Packard salesman. The program was supported by news releases and space advertising. The direct mail package was made up of a 9 × 12-

inch envelope, a letter, an eight-page capability report, a four-color brochure, a 3-D pop-up of the product to show its size, and an order card.

Another widely used tool of industrial communications is the exhibit. This most often takes the form of a showing at a trade show or convention.

At trade shows, exhibits are the primary reason for the shows. They provide an opportunity for manufacturers to show their products to audiences that are largely their customers. An example is the giant National Association of Home Builders trade show held every year. There products used in building homes are exhibited and can be sold right at the booths.

In the case of conventions, such as the huge Institute of Electrical and Electronic Engineers national meetings, the exhibits are usually a secondary reason for the event. But they do provide income for the sponsoring societies and associations. Such sponsors often prohibit selling in the exhibit hall.

Companies rent a specified amount of floor space from the organization sponsoring a trade show or convention. The sponsor rents the space from a hotel or convention center. The companies prepare their own exhibits and ship them to the place they are to be used.

The area a company rents, called a booth, is used to illustrate and demonstrate the company's products or services. Exhibitors continually compete with each other for the attention of the people attending the show. They keep looking for new ways to draw people into their booths. Some of the standard methods are pretty girls, games of various kinds (usually built around products or their features), things that move or bedazzle, skits and performances, and films.

Salesman and sometimes engineers man such booths. In the case of a highly complicated piece of equipment, such as a computer-controlled machine tool, an engineer may be needed to answer very technical questions.

Sales literature in an exhibit booth is a must. One of the primary reasons people attend such shows is to obtain product information. They want, and need, printed material that they can take away with them.

Cards are usually provided for visitors to the exhibit on which they can write their names and addresses. There is usually some incentive, such as a small gift or a raffle, to help people make up their minds to fill out a card.

Company publications distributed outside the company are yet another industrial communications tool. They run the gamut from simple newsletters to large-format, four-color, slick magazines. The latter are usually used by large companies to help maintain or build their images. But even small companies often have a newsletter type of company publication which is generally oriented toward the application of the company's products and services. There are many excellent publications of this kind in highly competitive and high-volume-production fields such as electronics.

COMMUNICATIONS SCHEDULE
Product XL-13 Welder

		Publicity	Space Advertising	Sales Literature
1975	January	New product announcement keyed to NADA trade show—mail January 15		
	February			
	March	New literature announcement	*National Automobile Dealers Assn. Journal*—obtain reprints	Sales letter, brochure, data sheet, catalog sheet—by March 1
	April			
	May	Commission public works case history May 1		
	June		*Automotive Dealers Monthly*—obtain reprints	
	July	Commission automotive case history July 15		Application notes #1 by July 1
	August	Public works case history publication in *American Municipality*—reprint		
	September			
	October	Commission industrial case history October 1		
	November	Automotive case history published in *Automotive Dealers Monthly*—reprint	*Public Works*—obtain reprints	
	December			
1976	January	Industrial case history published in *Manufactur-Engineering*—reprint	*American Municipalpality*—obtain reprints	Application notes #2 by January 1
	February			
	March			
	April		*Industrial Engineer*—obtain reprints	
	May	Commission farm equipment case history May 1		
	June	Commission mass transit case history June 1	*Manufacturing Engineering*—obtain reprints	
	July			Application notes #3 by July 1
	August	Farm equipment case history published in *Farm Equipment News*—reprint		
	September			
	October	Mass transit case history published in *Transportation*—reprint	*Farm Equipment News*—obtain reprints	
	November			
	December		*Farm Equipment News*—obtain reprints	Application notes #4 by December 1

Figure 4-2   Communications schedule and action plan.

Trade Shows	Direct Mail	Field Sales Aids and Literature	Company Newsletter
		Slide show and presentation to salesmen and reps, February 1	
National Automobile Dealers Association Meeting and Show March 18–22	Sales letter, brochure, data sheet, catalog sheet, reply card, March 15 mail	Sales letter, brochure, data and catalog sheets, NADA ad reprint	New product announcement
	Follow-up sales letter, data sheet, *NADA Journal* ad reprint *Automotive Dealers Monthly* ad reprint Second follow-up sales letter, data sheet, application notes #1	*Automotive Dealers Monthly* ad reprint Application notes #1	Application notes #1 Public works case history
American Public Works Association	Public works case history reprint *Public Works* ad reprint	Public works case history reprint *Public Works* ad reprint	Automotive case history
American Association of Industrial Engineers	Automotive case history reprint Application notes, *American Municipality* ad reprint Industrial case history reprint *Industrial Engineer* ad reprint	Automotive case history reprint Application notes, *American Municipality* ad reprint, new presentation, slides; industrial case history reprint *Industrial Engineer* ad reprint	Industrial case history Application notes #2
	Manufacturing Engineer ad reprint Application notes #3	*Manufacturing Engineer* ad reprint Application notes #3	Application notes #3 Farm equipment case history
National Association of farm equipment Dealers Meeting, October 28–November 3	Farm equipment case history reprint *Farm Equipment News* ad reprint	Farm equipment case history reprint *Farm Equipment News* ad reprint	Mass transit case history
Mass Transit Society of America Meeting, December 3–7	Application notes, *Farm Equipment News* ad reprint	Application notes, *Farm Equipment News* ad reprint	Application notes #4

Figure 4-2 (*Continued*)

Effective Use of the Tools

Perhaps the best way to show how the tools can be used together effectively in a carefully planned program is by using an example. The schedule and action matrix shown in Figure 4–2 is an oversimplified and fictitious example of a program on a hypothetical new welding product.

It should be recognized at the outset that the example plan is oriented toward supporting product sales in a company that manufactures relatively simple and low-cost products in large volume by traditional methods. Different companies must of course have different plans. And the plan for a company such as a management consulting firm would be much different. The communications program would be designed to help sell the firm's service, experience, and special knowledge. (It should be noted that planning, consulting, and other professional concerns usually do not advertise. The professional organizations to which they belong almost in all cases have some kind of sanction against advertising.) The communications program for a professional firm would be aimed toward building the concern's reputation as an organization that can solve the problems of other companies or of governmental bodies. The program would attempt to build recognition and stature, or image, rather than help sell products.

To return to the example communications program, it is assumed that the welder will go into production in March 1975, and that one of the first units off the assembly line will be shown at the National Automobile Dealers Association (NADA) meeting and show which takes place late in March.

The first element of the communications program is a new product announcement press release schedule for mailing January 15. Most of the target publications for the story are monthlies. So mailing on January 15 assures that February coverage will be minimized, since the February issues of most monthlies are usually finalized and in the process of being printed by January 15th. The press release will be keyed to the March showing of the welder at the NADA show; the monthlies will run the product announcement in their March issues.

Keying of the press release can be done one of two ways. It can be mentioned in the release, or a "note to editors" can be attached to the release giving the information about the welder being shown for the first time. Such a note could be attached to all the releases or just to those that go to publications that might cover the show.

The second element of the program is a slide show and presentation material which is to be sent to the company's salesmen and manufacturer's representatives by February 1 to give them time to familiarize themselves with the sales strategy before the introduction of the product. If the company has regularly scheduled sales meetings for its salesmen and representatives, the product should be introduced to them there. Another way companies sometimes go about familiarizing their salesmen and representatives with a product is to conduct training sessions either in the field or at the plant. In the case of the welder introduction, this probably is not necessary if the sales people are familiar with welding equipment. If, however, the XL-13 is completely different from the rest of the company's products, the sales people will have to be briefed in order to do an effective sales job.

In looking down the publicity column, it can be seen that the company is relying on case history articles written especially for certain publications as the publicity tool—afer the initial new product release and a literature announcement on the brochure—to carry the product message to the potential users.

The reason the case histories are shown spread out across two years is a practical one. Most companies do not have a writer who devotes all his time to case histories. Writers who produce publicity are usually involved in many other tasks such as working on company publications, sales literature, proposals, speeches, letters for executives, and so on. And if the writer works only on publicity, he probably is responsible for servicing other products or product lines in addition to the XL-13 welder. So the internal case history writer, If there is one, must allocate his time.

If there is no internal case history writer, these projects must be framed out to free-lance writers or to agencies. This is not inexpensive, and the communications money must be used for a variety of other tools in addition to case histories. This too is a reason for spacing the case histories.

Publication of the case histories should be explored with the editors of the target magazine. If the editors are not interested or have other reasons for turning the idea down, then the next most appropriate magazine should be contacted.

Types of case histories and how they are used are covered in more detail in Chapter 9. By comparing the publicity and advertising columns, it can be seen that the case histories are scheduled to appear in the same publications scheduled to carry advertising. The intent here is not to bribe the editor of the magazine with advertising. In most cases, it does not work. The case history stories have to be acceptable on their own merit. However, if a company advertises in a publication, the editor and publisher may be more receptive to the company's editorial offerings, especially if there is a surplus of good material from a variety of companies for the publication to choose from. L. Warren Lundgren, writing in *Industrial Marketing* magazine notes: "The publisher of an influential business publication is neither inclined nor obliged to trade articles for ads. Nor does he, on the other hand, appreciate running only your public relations material while you spend your advertising dollars in competitive publications."

In looking down the advertising column of the communications schedule, it can be seen that the company has decided to spread its advertising dollars over a range of publications. This may or may not be the best approach. Advertising experts say that repetition is a key factor in the effectiveness of advertising. Some say that five repetitions of an ad are necessary to achieve a respectable impact. The XL-13 welder ad is scheduled to appear only twice for each of the target audiences. For example, for the automotive audience, the ad is scheduled to appear both in the *NADA Journal* and the *Automotive Dealer's Monthly*—two appearances for approximately the same group of readers.

But here again, because of limited resources, a company or its product manager may elect to compromise in order to have a more balanced communications program. For some companies, this may not be a good policy. In some cases, when resources are inalterably limited, the wisest course may be to put all the eggs in one basket. Often, however, a lean though balanced program is preferable.

The items listed in the sales literature column are more-or-less standard material. The sales letter is a hard-sell tool used primarily in direct mail selling. The brochure is an attention-getting device using graphics, often color, and descriptive information on features and advantages. The data sheet gives the nitty-gritty characteristics and advantages, usually in technical language and through the use of charts, diagrams, schematics, tables, and the like. The catalog information is sometimes just the data sheet. In other cases, it may be part of a product line catalog and include information such as prices and discounts.

Application notes are brief, often one-page, descriptions of uses of a product. They are developed in a variety of ways. When a product is first put on the market, the applications foreseen for it are a result of the forecasts of engineers and marketing experts. Once a product reaches the marketplace, other applications often become apparent. They are suggested by field salesmen, application engineers, sales representatives, and customers. There are countless examples of unusual and profitable applications of products which were never dreamed of by the developers and marketers of the product.

The trade shows column is fairly straightforward. The company has decided to display the XL-13 welder in the specified trade shows. As previously indicated, the aim of the trade show or other exhibit is to place a product before an audience that includes a high percentage of possible users.

What is not specified in the trade show column is the information that will be available to hand out during the show. The brochures and data sheets will of course be part of the hand-out material. In almost every case, there will also be a reprint of a recent advertisement, a recent case history of interest to the visitors to the show, or both. This can be verified by looking back at the advertising and publicity columns in the schedule.

The direct mail category includes a sales letter and two follow-up sales letters. As mentioned above, sales letters are hard-sell selling tools which are designed, working with sales literature and a reply card, to elicit direct orders without the intervention of a salesman, or to elicit inquiries which can be pursued by a salesman. Also included in the direct mail column are the application notes and reprints of ads and published case histories.

All the direct mail information goes to selected potential customers or buying influences on mailing lists made up within the company or purchased or rented from any one of several firms that specialize in building and supplying mailing lists.

Field sales aids and literature are materials that salesmen and representatives will be able to use when they call on customers. Included in the example program in this category are a slide show and a written presentation the salesmen can refer to. These are periodically updated and improved. Also included in this category are all the sales literature, the application notes, and reprints of ads and published case histories.

The company newsletter included in the program publishes all the information disseminated that can be turned into editorial information. This includes the initial new product announcement, all the case histories, and the application notes. In such a program the newsletter is sent to all marketing and management people within the company, representatives outside the company, and customers on the direct mail lists.

The case histories used in the newsletter are intended to be published concurrently with publication in the target magazines. This should be negotiated in advance with the editors of the magazines. If the editors are not receptive of this, the company newsletter usage should be the one to suffer. But this will probably only mean that the newsletter story will appear later than the magazine article.

Effective use of the tools of communication within the framework of a total communications concept is difficult to achieve. In the complex and highly competitive business world of today, an outstanding communications job cannot be done for a company by communications specialists working independently. In many cases, it cannot even be done if everyone cooperates. The only real way to assure an effective job is by a type of teamwork that can be labeled synergistic.

In a valuable article, "Business Synergism: When 1 + 1 > 2," Robert

McManimie and William McGregor, writing in the August 1972 issue of *Innovation* magazine, gave some of the conditions for synergism:

* Perception of a need.
* Perception of a potentially effective response or possible solution.
* A change agent.

In order to build a synergistic group, McManimie and McGregor suggested the following requirements.

* A common cause.
* Policies of the group should be made by multifunction generalists.
* The group must have well-defined goals and yardsticks.
* Generalists in the group should be utilized to the maximum.
* Participation of specialists in policy making should be minimized.
* The group must have adequate resources.
* Disruptive factors must be minimized; cohesive factors maximized.

The focus of analysis should be on the *interaction* of people or of groups of concern, rather on than their individual behavior.

The subject of synergism is a fruitful approach to stimulating teamwork. But there are other approaches, and the important point to consider is that teamwork is essential to effective use of the tools of communications.

REFERENCES

John F. Budd, Jr., *An Executive's Primer on Public Relations*, Chilton Book Company, Philadelphia, Pa., 1969.

J. Warren Lundgren, "Customer-Authors Create Autocon Publicity," *Industrial Marketing*, January 1965, p. 89.

Robert McManimie, William McGregor, "Business Synergism: When 1 + 1 > 2," *Innovation*. August 1972.

Ted J. McLaughlin, Lawrence P. Blum, and David M. Robinson, *Communication*, Charles E. Merrill Books, Inc., Columbus, Ohio, 1964.

Bob Stone, "Direct Marketer Strikes it Rich with Direct Mail," *Advertising Age*, February 12, 1973.

5
THE INDUSTRIAL PUBLICITY ENVIRONMENT

INDUSTRY AND PUBLISHING INTERDEPENDENCE

One key to understanding the worlds of industry and publishing and how they relate to each other is the interdependence between them. The vast majority of publications are supported by advertising money which comes from industry and business. Industry depends on business and technical publications for information and guidance. Industry also depends on these publications to deliver information about products and services to many of its markets.

Publications are also dependent on industry for a steady stream of information. Much of the editorial information in these publications originates from industry, or is supplied by industry on request. *Business Week* magazine once remarked, "The simple fact is that much of the current news coverage of business by the American press, radio, and television are subsidized by company PR efforts." The magazine, of course, did not mean a direct monetary subsidy, but a subsidy in terms of supplying information and cooperating with the press.

Another role that publications fulfill—a role that is necessary but which sometimes causes industry to chafe—is to act as a sort of conscience, sometimes to the extent of playing devil's advocate.

Industry publicity people and journalists get along fairly well. In most cases, they understand each other and respect each other's positions. When their roles come into conflict, they usually try to avoid a heated confrontation.

There is one myth about the relationship between industry and the press that seems to persist. John Fisher, writing in *Harper's*, tried to lay this myth to rest. He said, "The legend that advertisers dictate the policy of newspapers and magazines is deeply imbedded in American folklore, and apparently has become an article of faith with the New Left. In fact, advertisers seldom attempt anything of the kind, and virtually never succeed."

The reasons why advertising does not greatly influence the editorial policies of publications is a bit complicated. In order to consistently attract advertising, a publication must have a base of loyal readers. The publication must be able to prove to advertisers that its readership not only receives it, but also reads it and places faith in the information printed. But readers are not naturally loyal to a publication. Their loyalty must be earned. The publication must run material the readers find interesting and useful. Otherwise, readers and potential readers will not subscribe to a publication or buy it at a newsstand.

So to win the loyalty of a readership, a publication must determine the needs of a readership and provide relevant information which helps fulfill these needs. How a publication goes about providing the needed information is determined by its editorial policies. These policies also determine the editorial qualities of a publication. If these qualities consistently attract readers, the publication has a creditable story to tell advertisers. So it is editorial policies, formulated on the basis of the editor's knowledge of his readership, that largely determine how well a publication attracts advertisers. In other words, editorial policies come first; advertising follows, not the other way around. In the final analysis, editorial characteristics determine whether or not a publication will be around to carry advertising.

The characteristics that determine if a publication survives are, according to William D. Lanier, a McGraw-Hill publisher, five in number. In a speech before a meeting of the American Business Press, he identified these characteristics as:

1. *Usefulness.* "If the editorial emphasis is on news, the news must be truly and directly significant, meaningful and useful to the reader. If the emphasis is on technology, the technical material must be selected from the whole surging expanse of technology and presented in directly useful terms to the specialist reader."

2. *Guidance.* There must be "reliable guidance as to the meaning of the news," and in the area of technology, "in telling the reader what he does not know and needs to know."

3. *Brightness.* This quality is the "ability to make the reader's effort at self-education an adventure—the ability to teach with excitement, enthusiasm and style."

4. *Personalization.* This means "attention to the reader as an individ-

ual—the ability to, and the willingness, to recognize and reassure him as a special and important individual."

5. *Force.* This refers to editorial force exerted to make the publication a "courageous critic, a forthright spokesman, an acknowledged leader in its field."

6. *Life.* This is characterized as the ability to make a useful and responsible publication also "alert, alive and lively, and a prime source of interesting shop talk."

Publications are judged—sometimes consciously by advertisers, sometimes unconsciously by readers deciding what they want to read—on their editorial quality. This judgment is highly subjective and sometimes very difficult. Byron K. Ledgerwood, while editor of *Control Engineering* magazine, gave in a speech a set of questions to aid in determining editorial quality. These are:

1. Editorial staff and its initiative.

- Are the editors experienced and educated in the field the publication serves?
- Do the editors know their readers and the industry that serves the readers?
- Do the editors dig for stories or do they wait for the stories to come to them?

2. Job done for the reader.

- Does the publication serve its readers first and foremost?
- Does it show the true profile of the field or does it parrot the line of its influential advertisers?

3. Credence and accuracy.

- Is the publication consistently accurate?
- Does it avoid the publication of attention-getting but unfounded rumors?
- Does it evaluate new developments and techniques in relation to their actual present and future significance?

4. Leadership.

- Is the publication the spokesman for its field?
- Does it offer worthwhile advice and criticism regardless of who's toes it steps on?

- Does it stimulate the reader with new ideas or only describe existing well-established practice?

INDUSTRY TRENDS AND CHARACTERISTICS

Changes in Industry

The influence of change was explored in Chapter 1. As pointed out there, numerous forces and pressures have been at work to cause changes in industry. These changes are occurring at an accelerating rate. They have been brought about by many things. Among them are elements of social expectation and awareness such as consumerism and environmentalism. Political changes are also part of the pattern. Within industry, changes have come about because of the pressure of labor unions and problems such as high absentee and turnover rates. Modern management methods based on findings of modern-day social science have led to more enlightened supervision of both blue- and white-collar workers.

Changes have also resulted from the conglomeration tendency of the recent past. Companies have been diversifying, acquiring other companies at a dizzying rate in an attempt to achieve a broader, more stable base and to realize the benefits of economy of scale. And with competition forcing the adoption of new and better machines and techniques, complexity has increased drastically. Finally, the asymptotic increase in new knowledge and its application has also forced changes.

Limiting Characteristics in Industry

Change demands an ability to respond to problems and opportunities dynamically, with flexibility and rapidity of action. But there are limitations on the ability to respond, caused largely by traditional industrial conservatism, by bureaucratic inertia, by the technocratic approach, and by obsolete organizational structures and management methods.

These limitations sometimes make it hard to obtain a decision quickly enough to make an effective response on matters in which public interest is involved.

A variety of influences comes under the label of industrial conservatism. It includes remnants of the laissez faire approach to doing business, a tendency not to speak out on public matters, and deferral of difficult decisions not directly related to the business at hand, which are usually the technical problems of manufacturing and selling products.

All organizations have some bureaucratic inertia, even small ones. Some of course are worse than others. In many instances, the making and communicating of decisions is agonizingly slow because the communications channels are long, circuitous, and clogged with paper.

Because of the complexity of doing business and because of the importance of technology in industry, many industrial executives have engineering or other technical backgrounds. Many of these executives tend to feel that problems—including public ones—can be solved by the use of impersonal systems and professional management techniques. But trying to systematize and quantify can be carried only so far in a function such as publicity which is mostly art and not much science. Work can sometimes be impeded by too great a stress on the technical approach.

Organization structures that are obsolete can also reduce the ability to respond to needs and opportunities. Some companies with the traditional pyramid hierarchy have found their organizations cannot react quickly and effectively enough to changing conditions. The pyramid structure also isolates parts of the organization from each other. For example, if one department wants the help of another, the request usually goes not to the other department but up the chain of command until an executive is reached to whom both departments report. Then the request descends in another channel, providing it has not been denied somewhere along the way, until it reaches its destination.

This process is a means of assuring that requests, or in other cases recommendations, are appropriate and in the best interests of the company. It also assures that things are done properly, because it brings requests and recommended actions under the scrutiny of experienced and competent people. But it also encourages a certain amount of fragmentation and alienation. Anthony Jay cites an example in *Corporation Man*:

There was a computer firm with three different types of staff who called on customers: the salesman to interest them in replacing or extending the configuration, the maintenance engineers to repair and service the equipment, and the software representatives to talk about applications. All of them worked independently and came under different divisions with a consequence that any experienced corporation man could foresee without being told: the maintenance man privately told the customer that the equipment was at fault, the salesman mentioned (off the record) that it would have been all right if properly maintained, and the software representative excused all failures in application by implying that the salesman had claimed a capacity of performance which was beyond the powers of the equipment and the programs.

Not only did the three men not work together, they were to an extent working against each other. And this example, although it is an extreme one, shows how there can be not only a lack of cooperation, but sometimes even competition of a destructive or antisynergistic nature.

The command and control benefits of the pyramid structure generally outweight the alienation and fragmentation problem. But the problem remains, and may be one of the root causes of severe financial difficulties of some major corporations.

Some innovations in organization have been tried in the recent past, but it may be too early to tell if they work. The major alternative to the pyramid organization is a "flat" structure in which operating managers all report to the chief executive officer rather than through a pyramid of vice-presidents and executive vice-presidents. This method has been tried in Europe and has been adopted by the dynamic new president of Kaiser Aluminum and Chemical Corporation, according to the February 24, 1973, issue of *Business Week* magazine. The flat organization permits faster decision making and leads to more involvement of all the managers in problems, objectives, and decisions.

Role of Competition

But industry is aware of limiting factors and tries to evolve new methods. The main pressure forcing this is economic competition. When a company or a part of a company begins doing badly in the way of profit and loss, its board of directors or president looks for reasons and solutions. Changes are made in personnel, organization, or ways of doing business to make the company more profitable.

One evolving tendency is an increased use of publicity to help make a company more profitable and competitive. And modern managers have gained much of their experience at a time when increased sensitivity to public attitudes has been necessary. So the expectations and attitudes with which they view the role of publicity are increasingly sophisticated.

Another form of competition that is becoming a more serious problem for publicity practitioners is competition for editorial space. One of the reasons for this is an increase in the number of suppliers. There are more companies and public relations agencies than ever before. Another reason is a growing awareness of the usefulness of publicity and a consequent increase in its use by established companies. Yet another reason is the growing communications problem. People are bombarded from all sides by messages from different media. Communications channels are becoming more crowded.

The communications problem is related to complexity in today's world. This complexity is due partly to an increasing population and to its increasing number of possessions, but it is also due to technology. Alvin Toffler, in *Future Shock*, stated:

> Each new machine or technique, in a sense, changes all existing machines and techniques, by permitting us to put them together into new combinations. The number of possible combinations rises exponentially as the number of new machines or techniques rises arithmetically. Indeed, each new combination may, itself, be regarded as a new super machine.

MEDIA CHARACTERISTICS AND TRENDS

There are innumerable ways publications can be characterized. A breakdown that may be useful here is:

- General media.
- Specialized consumer media.
- Specialized industrial media.
- Business and financial media.
- Newsletters.
- Professional media.

General media means newspapers, general magazines such as newsweeklies, radio, and television. Specialized consumer media are usually magazines, for audiences who share an avocational interest such as boating, fashion, or photography. Specialized industry publications are designed for audiences who share vocational interests such as the design and construction of ships, building of homes, or operating fleets of cars and trucks. Most newsletters are also directed to common-interest audiences but differ from the above specialized publications in that most carry no advertising. Their publishing costs are in most cases completely financed by subscriptions. There are now over 2000 commercial newsletters in the United States.

Professional publications are directed at audiences with very narrow specializations. They are often very technical and in many cases scholarly. Many carry advertising; some none at all. Many are subsidized by a professional association or society.

A useful comparison of media types can be made by looking at the two extremes of publicity information, image-related news and product information. The following matrix draws such a comparison.

	Image-Related News	Product Information
General media	Used if newsworthy to the general public	Rarely used unless it represents something like a breakthrough
Specialized consumer media	Used if newsworthy to the special-interest audience	Often used
Specialized industrial media	Used if newsworthy to its special-interest audience	Nearly always used
Business and financial media	Used if newsworthy to the financial community	Rarely used unless it represents something like a breakthrough
Newsletters	Used if newsworthy to its readers	Sometimes used
Professional media	Rarely used	Rarely used

General Media

The subject of general media can be further subdivided into the classifications of electronic media and printed media.

Electronic Media

The electronic media, television and radio, are extremely hard to interest in a business story. In a recent speech, Robert Goralsky, an NBC correspondent, talked about what is probably the best way to attract the attention of television and radio producers. That is simply to get something used by the wire services. This is a very strong factor in decisions on what information is used by the electronic media.

Television and radio do not lend themselves to explanation of complicated issues, problems, or systems. The capsulated news treatment of the predominant half hour news shows on television and the 5-minute news reports on most radio stations do not allow time for in-depth interpretive reporting. Another aspect of television reporting is that it is oriented toward controversy and action that can be depicted visually. Both television and radio insist upon one "actuality" or more in their news reports.

Actualities are statements made to correspondents or television pictures showing action.

General Printed Media

Television is challenging the general printed media—newspapers and general magazines—for the attention of the people who want news. But although more than half these people claim that television is their primary source of news, the printed media is probably still the most influential. The time alloted to a news story on television, which is typically 2 1/2 minutes or less, is not enough time to give more than a cursory report which is usually vastly oversimplified. Newspapers and magazines are able to delve more deeply into the news. This brings many if not most people back to the printed media for an understanding, not just a brief report, of events that are making news.

Newspapers and magazines are well aware of such trends, and have shifted somewhat from news presentation toward more investigative and interpretive reporting. The electronic media are doing less of this type of reporting all the time. The number of hours of documentary programs on television continues to decline.

There is, however, no doubt that television has made viewers out of a lot of readers. This is one factor in the reduction of the number large metropolitan dailies that has been, and still is, going on. Television is also held partly responsible for the demise of the large-format, photo-oriented magazines *Look* and *Life*.

Another cause for a reduction of the number of newspapers and magazines is simply economics. The costs of information gathering, production, and distribution continue to rise steeply.

Under the pressure of competition from television, the general printed media have brightened their coverage and made it more relevant. As a consequence, they have become less receptive to the flood of industry-supplied material. Press releases have become a less effective way of obtaining coverage. Personal contact of journalists with professional communicators has become the best—and in many cases the only—way of obtaining coverage. There are, however, two rather narrow areas where press releases are still welcomed. One is the shopping columns that some newspapers, Sunday supplements, and magazines run. The other is the financial or business section of a newspaper.

Specialized Media

The five other types of publications listed above—specialized consumer, specialized industrial, business and financial, newsletters, professional—can be grouped together somewhat arbitrarily under the category of specialized press.

As a group, these publications are not completely compatible. But from the viewpoint of the publicity practitioner, the methods of working with this group are similar in all five types.

Specialized publications are read by people who have something in common. This may be a type of business such as a retail hardware store, a profession such as medicine, a trade such as plumbing, or a hobby such as photography. The reason most readers want these publications is to help them do something better or make it more interesting.

The readers of specialized publications are in a sense all experts of one type of another. Sid Bernstein, in a column in *Industrial Marketing* magazine, brought this into focus in some remarks about an editor of this type of publication, who, he said, "talks to people who not only know what they're talking about; they know what he's talking about, too—and this creates an atmosphere that screens out the insignificant and the half-right, and at the same time develops a rapport between editor and reader which it is almost impossible to achieve in consumer media."

The specialized consumer segment of the publishing business has grown remarkable in the recent past. Chris Welles, writing in the *Columbia Journalism Review*, pinpointed the reason: "Higher levels of affluence, education, and leisure time have permitted people to develop and exploit individual interests, tastes, and capabilities. This in turn has produced a growing fragmentation of the mass audience and the mass media." He goes on to say that the financially most successful magazines of the past 10 years "have been designed to appeal to highly particularized, vocational, and avocational interests and are run by editors who know precisely what they are saying and to whom they are saying it."

An illustration of the effectiveness of specialized publications from the viewpoint of the advertiser was provided by A. R. Roalman in *Writer's Digest*. He said that an advertisement in *Mobile Home Journal* "greatly outpulled the total return from a similar ad in regional editions of *TV Guide* with a circulation of 2,000,000 and one on network television. *Mobile Home Journal* then had a circulation of about 55,000."

The time of the specialized consumer publications has definitely arrived. Large-circulation magazines which were unable to segment their readership demographically lost out to specialized publications or to those that were able to apply demographics and segment. Some such as the *Saturday Evening Post, Look,* and *Life,* went out of business at least partly for this reason. Some other high-circulation general magazines such as *Harper's, New Yorker,* and *Holiday* slipped in circulation.

Trade, industrial, and business publications have been published on a demographic basis for a long time. But even so, over the past few years, publications that did not do a good job of pinpointing their readership suffered. And some went under when the economic crunch came in 1969–1971. That was when overall advertising revenues dropped 8 percent while costs drastically increased. Over the decade of the 1960's, mailing costs increased 110 percent, staff salaries rose by 60 percent, and printing costs went up about 30 percent. Inflation of these costs occurred at a much higher rate in the publishing business than inflation in the country as a whole.

Specialized magazines have grown in number and profitability. From the economic standpoint, the reason they are doing so well is that they are able to give their advertisers exact information on the nature of their readership. This enables the advertisers to direct their commercial messages to exactly the audience they want to reach. The cost per thousand readers of advertising space—the standard method of gauging advertising expense— may be higher in a small circulation specialized publication, but the advertiser is confident that his message at least reaches the right audience. Although the readership of a general magazine might include the target audience, there is no way of knowing for sure whether the right readers are exposed to the message unless the circulation is segmented.

The readership of most specialized publications is well defined. And there are organizations set up especially to audit circulations to assure that advertisers are getting the most for their money. But one problem that sometimes arises is that there may be too many specialized publications in a field. Eventually, of course, magazines that are not reaching their readers with the kind of information they want and need go out of business or change their editorial approach to appeal to a different set of readers. But before this shaking-out process occurs, there may be a glut on the market, so to speak. In such a situation, the advertiser is not getting the most "bang for a buck."

Although it is necessary that a specialized publication carefully define its audience and provide it with relevant information, this is not sufficient. If the target audience does not control expenditures for products or services, the publication may not attract enough advertising to be self-supporting.

Specialized magazines, especially industrial publications, are dependent on the industry they are associated with. When economic conditions in an industry worsen, advertising budgets are the first to be cut and specialized publications are hardest hit.

The economic picture for specialized, and general publications as well, is further clouded by fewer advertising dollars "per capita." Conditions in the recent past have seen the slowing of the rate of increase in advertising money available. Additional complicating factors are the increasing sophistication of advertisers and increased competition in the publishing industry.

Influence of Advancing Technology

The effect of new advancements in information methods and equipment was neatly summarized in a brochure recently disseminated by McGraw-Hill Publications Company. In part, it said:

> As we move into fully computerized editorial composition on our magazines—which will eventually involve computer storage of all editorial matter—we envision the 'repackaging' of the vast quantities of information and data we can retrieve electronically. Ultimately, wholly new media, some of them electronic, will evolve from this growing capability. Some are on our drawing boards now.

Technological innovations are being put into practice in response to various pressures. The dominant factor is the geometric increase in the volume of information—the so-called information explosion—which is proliferating at a fantastic rate. This in turn has forced individuals to try to find ways of separating the wheat—the information they want and need—from vast amounts of chaff. As a consequence, forms of information services competitive with traditional methods are being developed and pressed into service.

The written word will most probably always be with us. Thinking is done with words, and people learn these words by using both their visual and auditory senses. In addition, there is no known substitute for selective review of written records. This allows an individual to rapidly scan written material and to quickly go back over a sentence or a section. So the big changes that come about because of advanced technology will not result in elimination of the written word, but in changes in the way words are stored and retrieved for use.

Despite the usefulness of the written word, the conventional conveyors of information—magazines and newspapers—are a roundabout and expensive way of getting information to people. A complicated series of events must be completed successfully and on time to transfer the information from source to reader. Publications can at best provide bits and pieces of useful information periodically to some, hopefully most, of their readership.

Another disadvantage publications have from the viewpoint of the reader is the presence of advertising and useless information which, first, must be scanned and rejected, and second, distracts attention. Such material interferes with the reader's finding the information he is after.

So new ways of conveying information to "users" are being developed. And some publications are already being affected.

The publications most vulnerable to competition from the new media are those that carry information of a very specific nature. Some examples are information on product data, design techniques for engineers, and theater tickets. Publications that will be least affected are those that appeal to reader characteristics that cannot be easily profiled. Examples of such characteristics are intellectual curiosity, a philosophical bent, a desire to be entertained while being informed.

So publications in general are having to shift their editorial approaches away from information that can be stored in data banks toward interpretive and analytical reporting. Instead of just supplying information readers want—a role data banks are increasingly fullfilling—publications must give readers information they do not know they need, as well as interpretation.

Some possible new informational methods that may in part replace publications are:

- Display using a conventional television receiver.
- Facsimile reproduction using a cable terminal.
- Computer terminal with a printer or visual display.
- Teletype.
- Television and radio tapes.
- Microfilm and microfiche.
- Telephone with a television display.

Whatever mixture of methods eventually results, electronics is sure to dominate. But the precise form electronic information will take is not yet clear. It is certain, however, that in the not-too-distant future all experts will have access to computer-stored information of a specific nature. Laboratories, engineering centers, institutions, businesses and even homes will have terminals. These will allow access to computer networks, eventually on a continental and even a global scale. Such networks will provide virtually all known information that can be stored and retrieved.

But information and retrieval are not the only considerations. The nature of the inputs is also important. If the information is useless or in a form that defies retrieval, there is obviously no point in storing it. For example, there are legions of abstractions in scientific literature that cannot be applied to specific problems. Countless theories have been developed and in most cases stated in mathematical formulas. But the work necessary to apply most of the theories and formulas has not yet been done. So they are useless to a designer or technician looking for a solution to a practical problem.

REFERENCES

Sid Bernstein, "Some Inside Dope on Business Papers," *Industrial Marketing*, June 1964.

Business Publication Rates & Data, Standard Rate & Data Service, Inc., Skokie, Ill., 1973.

John Fischer, "The Perils of Publishing: How to Tell When You Are Being Corrupted," *Harper's*, May 1968.

Robert Goralsky, "Media Man's View of Aerospace," speech delivered to Aerospace Industries Association Public Affairs Council Meeting, April 3, 1973.

William D. Lanier, "The Publisher's View of Editorial Values," speech delivered to the Editorial Session of the American Business Press Winter Conference, March 1, 1967.

Byron K. Ledgerwood, "Editorial/Public Relations Interfaces," speech delivered to the Eastern New England Chapter Meeting of the Association of Industrial Advertisers, February 7, 1963.

"Public Relations Today" *Business Week*, July 2, 1960.

A. R. Roalman, "Davis Publications: 23 Markets at One House," *Writer's Digest*, November 1966.

"Swinging into the Seventies," McGraw-Hill Publications Company, New York, 1969.

6

INDUSTRIAL PUBLICITY
PLANNING CONSIDERATIONS

INTRODUCTION TO PLANNING

It is probably safe to say that most publicity is not part of a well-planned program. Even though there are cases in which one or more publicity tools can be used effectively on a one-shot or limited basis, a program approach makes much more sense. This means that publicity is used on a continuing basis in concert with other communications tools such as advertising. Such programs need a lot of detailed planning.

Planning that is more or less formal eliminates a lot of the guesswork that must otherwise be done. Operating by guesswork admittedly sometimes works. But it is not efficient because it results in a lot of wheel spinning and even mistakes. Also, this method of working does not lend itself to evaluation as well. If the objectives are not clearly spelled out, they cannot be realistically assessed, and undefined goals cannot be measured.

Most forms of industrial planning are geared to stepwise programs which result in developing, manufacturing, building selling, or buying something. Formalized planning and follow-up methods such as PERT (*P*rogram *E*valuation and *R*eview *T*echnique) and CPM (*C*ritical *P*ath *M*ethod) are aimed at defining milestones and gearing activity to meet predetermined dates on the way to the milestones. Tasks within the program are defined, dates set for completion of the tasks—reaching the milestones—and individuals assigned formal responsibility for accomplishing tasks. Some users of these new methods are so sold on them that they feel the methods can be applied to any business or industrial process. One Los Angeles home builder, for example, uses CPM for scheduling advertising and publicity for his condominiums and other projects. This probably would not work for many communications programs.

Another important feature of formalized industrial planning is feedback.

Individuals responsible for tasks in the program are required to continually provide information on the progress of their part of the program.

Much can be borrowed from industrial planning to plan publicity programs. However, publicity programs usually cannot be planned as rigorously, because it is less of a science and more of an art. Still, the only professional thing to do is to formulate reasonable and realistic objectives and establish means of carrying them out.

In general, planning involves finding out where you stand, determining what has to be done, and identifying the best way to do it.

The three dimensions of industrial publicity planning are the objectives of a program, the audience to be reached, and the subjects to be talked about. The various aspects of these dimensions are developed to a considerable extent in this chapter and in Chapters 7 and 11.

Some of the key ideas in planning are listed below. Their exact interpretation and how they are put together in a particular program depends a lot on company and business environment factors. In whatever way they are interpreted, they represent most if not all of the interrelated functions that come into play in planning. The key ideas fall into two groups which represent opposite ends of a spectrum.

General, Long-Range, Abstract	Specific, Short-Range, Concrete
Program	Plan
Strategy	Tactics
Objectives	Goals
Opportunities	Projects
Priorities	Limitations
Evaluating	Reporting
Methods	Tools
Audiences	Media
	Publics

There is a lot of confusion about the distinction between programs and plans, objectives and goals, and strategy and tactics.

Strategy and tactics are the easiest to distinguish. They are borrowed from military terminology where they have very specific meanings. Strategy is planning and directing large-scale military operations and maneuvering forces prior to actual engagement. In industrial planning, this means action-oriented planning which takes place before the action begins, or which is removed from the place where the action is taking place.

Tactics is the military science of arranging and maneuvering military forces in action or before the enemy. In reality, this is probably more an art than a science. In industrial planning, it refers to workaday operations.

Program and plan are fairly easy to tell apart. A program implies a broad scope, long-range thinking, and looking at all sides. It requires action, usually a series of tasks to accomplish predetermined broad objectives. A plan is the formulation, usually written, of specific tasks to be done, the dates by which they must be done, and the individuals who are responsible for getting them done. An example of a plan is given in a later section.

Objective and goal are harder to distinguish. A clue to the distinction is in the *adjective* form of the word objective which means independent of the mind, actual, real. This implies that the *noun* form has overall, broad, long-range, impartial, impersonal connotations. Goal is more definite as to time and method. It might be considered a measurable objective.

DETERMINING BACKGROUND

The first step in the planning process is the initial spadework that determines where the company is at a particular point in time. Some of the areas that must be explored are various aspects of the organization, the people that must be dealt with, and the history of past publicity and other communications efforts. Information about these aspects must be gathered and classified.

Every organization is different. It is important to know who the movers and doers are; the organization chart is not the best quide to this. Another type of vital knowledge is how information flows through the organization. The policy and procedures guides do not always reflect the true channels and methods. Some organizations, especially smaller ones, operate with a minimum of paperwork. The bigger the company, the more forms, reports, and controls it has to have, and the easier it is to trace the channels. There is more of an ad hoc element in the channels and procedures in a smaller company.

The people involved in planning and carrying out a publicity program are crucial to its effectiveness. The people who are responsible for communications functions have to be identified. In one case, the president of a company may consider the functions important enough to involve himself in them directly. In another company, the responsibility may be delegated to a secondary or even a tertiary level of the organization. In one company, responsibility for all the functions may be vested in a single individual. In another company, responsibility may be divided among two or more individuals. In extreme cases, it may be diffused through the organization to the extent that it is difficult to trace.

Finally, it is important to find out what has been done in the past and how effective it was. There are at least two good reasons for this. It can show what has worked for the organization in the past. Also, it can reveal which, if any, of the previous measures failed, and may indicate if there are any sensitivities in the organization that have been carried over from previous programs. For example, it is good to know the why and how if the president oᶠ the company was raked across the coals in print after a diastrous interview, It would probably not be a good idea to suggest a similar interview.

This example points up the importance of attitudes in an organization to the effectiveness of a program. It is as important to monitor attitudes as it is to gather background data.

Although it is not directly a part of background determination, an attempt should be made during this phase to inform and educate, to build an awareness of the part publicity can play in fulfilling the public relations and marketing objectives of the company.

The following example is the body of a letter illustrating some of the elements of background determination. It is apparent that the writer has already done considerable work in determining the background, and that an ongoing program exists but is considered inadequate.

To get oriented for our annual publicity planning meeting on Thursday, Jim, I thought I ought to put down some thoughts on what needs to be done.

One of the objectives for next year is to attempt to work out a procedure for the stimulation and more efficient handling of signed articles. Comparatively few articles are originated in your department.

Another objective is to determine the priority of publicity projects in terms of over-all importance. This is consistent with the company communications objective of concentration on the areas with big potential and a big communications need.

I'm listing below the broad areas of your department's work as I see them. In our publicity planning, I propose to fit publicity projects into these categories in order of their importance. The first item of concern, then, is to make certain that these broad areas are correct.

Products and Services

- Oceanographic Systems
- Underwater Surveillance
- Manned Submersibles
- Life Support

Capability

- Ocean Engineering
- Applied Science
- Deep Submergence

Here are the things I need to establish, for each publicity project I work on, in order to keep on top of your department's publicity effort and to do the most effective job.

- Technological area and subject
- Publicity objectives
- Information coordinator
- Information source
- Kind of information or type of publicity project
- Timing
- Audience

Technological Area and Subject (e.g., underwater surveillance, ocean bottom scanning sonar).

Publicity Objectives. These normally are parallel to or at least support marketing objectives (e.g., help inform buying influences that your department has excellent capability for engineering deep submergence equipment).

Information Coordinator. Knowledgeable individual in marketing that has responsibility in the stated technological area. This individual supplies guidance both to me and to the information source. In this capacity, he is essential.

Information Source. The engineering or project manager who knows the subject and is in a position to either supply needed information or cause the information to be supplied.

Kind of Information or Type of Publicity Project. This is the publicity tool that is selected to accomplish the stated objective (e.g., article, new product announcement).

Timing. Time at which the publicity project should be initiated so that it can be released at the optimum time.

Audience. This is the customer or other group to which the publicity should be directed. The makeup of the desired audience partly determines the slant of the information and determines the publications to which it will be sent.

I'm convinced that an effective publicity job can only be done if an effective planning job is done first. The reasons for this are many but it is a demonstrated fact. We laid the groundwork for a publicity program last year and now that everyone at least recognizes its existence, we can continue its development.

DEFINING THE PLANNING APPROACH

The background information on the organization, the attitudes of its members, and past activity can be formally written up for future reference or for the guidance of others. Although the tendency usually is to retain the information in raw form, there is much to be said for the discipline of writing it up. It becomes more understandable and coherent, and may be useful later as part of a publicity or communications program.

The method to be followed in the planning process is defined using the background information. The main determinants are conditions and elements of the company, the marketplace, public attitudes, and the media. Some of the company elements are the nature of its products or services, and the type and level of its technology. Some of the important product considerations are volume, complexity, cost, time to produce, and sales turnover. Some of the marketplace elements are the nature and distribution of customers, the nature and extent of competition, and demand levels and cycles.

The two extremes of the planning approach are the project or one-shot basis and the overall company, division, or department program basis. The project basis is often used in crisis situations in an attempt to accomplish some limited objective. It is probably safe to say that in most cases crisis-oriented publicity projects are too late to do any good. In one such project, the price of a small company's stock was plummeting. In an attempt to reverse this, the company called a press conference in connection with a space flight and attacked a large company saying that they (the small company) had developed the technology used by the big company in obtaining a significant contract. Some of the less well-informed reporters and those looking for controversy reported on the press conference. The knowledgeable business writers would not touch it. In fact, the one primary business paper in which the small company very much wanted coverage refused even to show up at the press conference. It is reasonable to assume that the next time the business writers came across the name of the small company, they were sure to question whatever the company had to say.

The project basis can sometimes be used by itself to good effect, but this is mainly in the area of product publicity. Even product publicity is usually more effective when it is used in conjunction with capability publicity, and the latter usually requires more long-range, strategic planning. This in turn means the overall organization program basis.

Although every organization is different, in most cases the best approach is to formulate general objectives as an umbrella for a set of specific objectives or goals.

An important part of defining the planning approach is to determine the scope of the program, largely a matter of setting limits and boundaries. One of the considerations is the nature of the organization. The importance of this was pointed up in the previous section on background determination. It is important to know where the responsibility and authority for policy are located in the organization. How and where the publicity operation really fits in the organization is necessary information.

Another consideration influencing the scope is resources. It is good to have realistic information on how much manpower and money can· be devoted to the publicity effort. Direct time and cost can be determined without much difficulty. An estimation of indirect time and cost is harder to come by. This may include things such as engineers' time involved in gathering information or preparing write-ups, travel expense for executives, arrangements and preparations—items of expense or time that are charged to overhead or to a budget other than that of the publicity operation.

As this implies, it is sometimes possible for a publicity manager to try actively to make use of many resources other than his own manpower and money. But within the organization this has to be handled carefully to avoid antagonizing other activities.

Yet another scope consideration is the type of material to be handled and the types of activities the publicity operation will become involved with. As a practical matter, out of the long list of publicity tools and techniques, it is doubtful that a particular publicity operation is involved in all of them all the time. For example, in many organizations, technical articles and papers are handled separately from press releases. The engineering department in many companies considers technical information one of its areas of responsibility, while the marketing department takes care of press releases. In some companies, speeches for executives are handled by the general management administrative staff, and so on.

At some point, any discussion of information gathering and decision making in an organization has to deal with the subject of meetings. Most people have mixed feelings about meetings, and rightly so. On the one hand, meetings are the only good way of accomplishing certain kinds of things. But when conditions are not right, meetings can also be a monstrous waste of time.

Meetings can be held on a periodic or called basis. The periodic type are held on a regular basis, and everyone involved understands the purpose and what they are expected to contribute. The Friday morning staff meeting falls into this category. Called meetings are scheduled in response to a new need or opportunity.

For publicity planning, a combination of periodic and called meetings is useful. The publicity manager should sit down on a regular basis with the organization's executives to discuss priorities and new needs and opportunities. This also gives him a chance to talk about progress and make recommendations on things he sees that need to be done. Called meetings should be used as necessary when significant events come about that affect the publicity program.

An all-important influence on the effectiveness of meetings is how they are organized. At one end of the spectrum is the highly structured meeting using an agenda. This is needed in cases in which most of the participants are not familiar with the subject and do not know each other. This type of meeting should be organized to start with basics and follow a natural progression toward accomplishing its purpose. At the other end of the spectrum is the highly informal meeting with no written agenda. This works effectively only when all the participants know each other well and know a lot about the subject of the meeting.

When meeting with an individual, especially an executive, it is a good idea to have something that concerns the subject to show him. It should be something simple like an outline. For example, if the intent of the meeting is to elicit from an executive the priority projects in his area of responsibility, he can be handed a list of items. He then can add to, delete from or change the list as he wishes. This puts the meeting on the right track immediately.

The important things usually discussed in planning meetings are objectives, strategy, themes, procedures, opportunities, scheduling, assignments of responsibility, priorities, problems, limitations, and reporting methods.

Two devices that can be both an agenda and a way of keeping track of information important to the eventual plan are the questionnaire and the matrix. These range from simple to detailed. Their exact makeup depends on several factors, among which are the level of technology involved in the area of interest, the degree of familiarity with the application of publicity on the part of everyone involved in the planning, and how such things are customarily handled in the organization.

Much, perhaps even most, of the time, the main value of a questionnaire or matrix is to serve as a guide to direct the discussion during planning meetings. It is often hard for a publicity man to keep discussions with executives on the track, and anything that helps put boundaries around the subject area of a meeting is helpful.

In the following examples, there are two questionnaires and two matrices. In each case, the first is simple and the second detailed.

It is important to note that these examples are just that, and that a questionnaire or matrix has to be tailored for a particular planning situation.

Here is an example of a simple questionnaire.

Date_____

Department_____

Objective:

Type of Information:

____Signed article   ____New product or service announcement

____Unsigned feature   ____New sales literature announcement

____Development release   ____Background information

Best time for appearance of information:_____

The following is an example of a detailed questionnaire.

PUBLICITY PLANNING FORM

Planned by: *Date:*

Subject:

____Author
   or
____Information source:

Type of Information:

____News release
   ____Announcement of development
   ____New product announcement
   ____New literature announcement
   ____Press background information
   ____Technical paper distribution
   ____Personnel announcement
   ____Facilities announcement
____Article
   ____Employe-written

_____Free lance-written
_____Press relations
_____Visit to editor
_____Press briefing
_____Supply information for staff-written article

Objective(s) Disseminate Information to:

_____Stimulate inquiries and requests by:

_____New product or service introduction press release
_____New product feature information
_____New sales literature announcement press release
_____Other:

_____Provide identification in a market by:

_____Describing significant development
_____Giving application information
_____Other:

_____Educate and inform customers and buying influences

_____Show competence and ability in:

_____Development engineering
_____Application engineering
_____Applied research
_____Basic research
_____Manufacturing
_____Management

_____Other:

Timing

_____is the best date or time period
for publication of this information.
Reason(s):

*Due Date:*_____

_____Outline or summary of proposed article.
_____News release information:

_____Specially prepared
_____Proposal or proposal summary
_____Technical paper

____Report
____Other:

Customer Audience(s):

____Industrial (give segment):
____Other:

Market Areas:

General:

    ____Aviation
    ____Defense
    ____Electric power
    ____Electronics
    ____Electrooptics
    ____Field engineering and service
    ____Manufacturing
    ____Marine
    ____Nuclear power
    ____Research
    ____Space
    ____Systems
    ____Other:

Specific:

    ____Communications
    ____Control
    ____Data management
    ____Display
    ____Electronic countermeasures
    ____Ground support equipment
    ____Guidance
    ____Missiles and rockets
    ____Navigation
    ____Oceanography
    ____Power conditioning
    ____Power conversion
    ____Power transmission
    ____Propulsion
    ____Radar, airborne
    ____Radar, ground
    ____Radar, shipborne
    ____Radar, space

____Sonar
____Surveillance/reconnaisance
____Test equipment
____Vehicles
____Other:

Techniques:

____Cryogenics
____Materials development
____Solid state electronics
____Packaging
____Process development
____Electrooptics
____Testing
____Computer-aided design
____Digital design

Missions:

____Scientific
____Strategic
____Tactical
____Exploratory

Here is an example of a simple matrix.

	Publicity Projects			
	1	2	3	4
Objective				
Subject				
Media				
Timing				

A more detailed matrix is the following:

	Immediate	Strategic	Emergent	International
Objective				
Opportunities				
Priorities				
Limitations and problems				
Timing considerations				
Publicity projects				

- Press relations
- Press releases
- Articles

There are of course many other ways to document information to be used in developing a plan. In its simplest form, it could be recorded in the form of a short memo. One of the possible patterns this might take is:

Meeting date.
Participants.
Background (needs, problems).
Objectives.
Audiences and media.
Opportunities and possibilities (candidate publicity projects).

Since planning generally does not take place in a vacuum, a final consideration in defining an approach is that planning is a continual, not an intermittent, process. Once a plan is developed, it will evolve as conditions change. This means it must be brought up to date from time to time. How often the plan should be updated depends on its extent and complexity, how dynamic the company's business is, and the type of product or service the company provides.

REFERENCES

George Black, *Planned Industrial Publicity*, Putnam Publishing Company, Chicago, Ill., 1952.

Raymond Simon, Ed., *Perspective in Public Relations*, University of Oklahoma Press, Norman, Okla., 1966.

B. W. Hoyle, *Information Services in Public Welfare Agencies*, WA Publication 19, Welfare Administration, U.S. Department of Health, Education and Welfare, U.S. Government Printing Office, Washington, D.C., 1960.

7

PLANNING INDUSTRIAL PUBLICITY

The previous chapter dealt with the preliminaries to planning. This chapter is devoted to the heart of the planning process, the determination of objectives and the formulation of a plan. What follows should not be taken as a how-to-do-it manual, but as a presentation of methods and approaches. There are two reasons for this. One is that the approach and the plan must fit the situation. Trade-offs and alternatives are always involved in tailoring an approach for a particular situation. A second reason is that if a publicity manager tried to put into practice every suggestion in this chapter, he might never finish planning, much less have time to implement the plans.

It may be useful at this point to reestablish a perspective of what general industrial publicity is and how it works. First, it has three main purposes:

- Support marketing objectives.
- Support public relations objectives.
- Press relations and information services.

The motivations for the support of marketing and public relations objectives are primarily internal. That is, they are conceived and initiated within an organization. The reasons for press relations and information services are partly internal and partly external. They are external in cases in which press representatives ask questions, and when an organization is trying to live up to what it feels is its obligation as a good citizen to make information about its activities available or to comply with the spirit of the freedom of information act. So it is necessary during planning to keep in mind both the internal and external needs and demands.

The operations of industrial publicity can be classified as:

- Plan.
- Implement plans.
- Evaluate results.

Planning can be further broken down:

- Determine objectives.
- Define the messages and the subjects.
- Establish timing.
- Define the publics and identify the media.
- Identify the tools and techniques.
- Draw up a plan of action.

ESTABLISHING OBJECTIVES

There are various ways of looking at objectives. One general way is to determine whether they are negative or positive. Objectives that deal with problems are negative, and those that deal with opportunities are positive. This is a fairly important distinction, since problems are usually tackled using a defensive approach, while opportunities are approached offensively. But in this as in other areas of human endeavor, the best defense is sometimes a good offense.

Another way of classifying objectives is by the organizational level at which they are formulated. It is extremely important to know or identify the proper level to avoid a severe case of confusion. The accompanying diagram indicates the various levels of objectives in a small company.

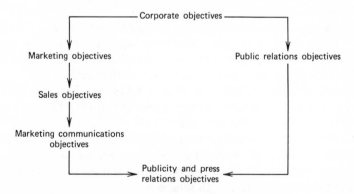

The foregoing applies to a low-technology, high-product-volume company. For the company or division at the other end of the spectrum, with a high technology content and a systems or research and development orientation, the levels of objectives might be:

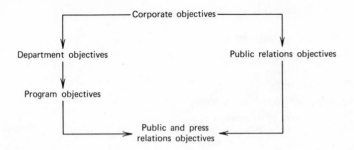

To help put in better perspective the nature of objectives, here are three examples:

- Support product sales with publicity.
- Demonstrate research and development capability through publicity to support sales indirectly.
- Demonstrate good corporate citizenship by publicizing the company's community activities.

The first two objectives are marketing support objectives; the third is a public relations objective.

Objectives do not stand alone as unrelated entities in the planning and implementation of publicity programs. They are the fulcrum of the publicity process.

The formulation of an objective is accomplished by stating it, testing its applicability, and modifying it as necessary.

The first step in the formulation is to state the objective in terms of the sales or public relations message to be imparted. The question that naturally follows is: To whom is the message to be directed? The answer to this question may cause the original objective to be modified.

Once the objective is stated so that it takes into account the publics involved, it must be considered in terms of the media. This may lead to another modification of the objective.

Yet another consideration in the formulation of objectives is appropriate subjects or opportunities. If it is not possible to identify a subject that will serve as the vehicle for the message, the objective must be changed or, when there is no other alternative, even scrapped.

Finally, the available and practical tools and techniques must be considered. In the worst case, there may be no feasible way of executing the plan that evolves from the objective. If this is so, the objective is unachievable and should be dropped or changed accordingly.

ESTABLISHING GOALS

Some practitioners use the term *specific objective* to describe what is described here by the word *goal*. (In that context, *objective* as it is used here becomes *general objective*.) It may seem to be a fine distinction, but there is a difference between a specific objective and a goal. The rationale for the distinction begins with the assumption that a goal is measurable. In some cases, however, especially in the area of public relations objectives, a measurable goal is an unobtainable ideal. In these cases, the concept of a specific objective should be used instead of the concept of a goal.

To say that a goal must be measurable does not necessarily mean that it *will* be measured. Most companies do not want to, or cannot, devote the manpower or money needed to measure each and every goal. Still, at some point it is desirable and sometimes necessary to make such measurements, if only on an occasional basis, to see if any real results are being obtained. Whether or not goals are measured consistently, it is a good practice to strive only for goals having results that can be quantified, where some meaningful number can be assigned in an evaluation of results.

The following are some typical goals. In comparing them to the objectives listed previously, it can be seen that these goals are much more specific. They include elements of timing and of quantitative results.

- Increase share of the widget market from 13 to 18 percent by the end of 1975.
- Double brand recognition among Japanese customers over the next year.
- By the end of 1974, reverse the proportion of customers (60 percent) who feel our products have quality inferior to that of our competitors. Conduct an opinion survey in early 1975 to determine if the goal has been met.
- Introduce the three new products that will emerge from development during the next 12 months.
- Introduce and stimulate meaningful inquiries on the new model of the widget, but limit dissemination so that only about 100 such inquiries will be received. (Expanded production facilities will not be completed for another 18 months. Meantime, we want to keep the product moving. Also, we will increase the sales effort gradually and initially will not be able to respond to large numbers of inquiries.)
- Reduce the cost of selling the widget line by 2 percent by increasing editorial coverage of the widget to precondition customers before the first sales contact.

- Demonstrate to the financial community how capable and stable the company is, so that the downward trend of the stock price can be reversed by July to pave the way for a new issue of stock a year later.

PLAN OF ACTION

As previously emphasized, there is no standard approach that fits every publicity planning situation. This is no less true of the writing of the plan. There are, however, several key considerations that must be taken into account whether or not they appear in the final plan.

The plan is the written expression of publicity ranging from far-reaching overall programs to specific publicity projects. It may take any of a variety of forms, and may be anywhere from one to dozens of pages in length.

From a practical viewpoint, there are two types of plans. One shows interested individuals what is going to be done, and the other serves as a guide to what will be done. They can be radically different. A plan used to show others what is to be done requires a lot of explanation and a more-or-less formal structure. A guide or working plan is usually some form of schedule.

A useful way to approach the plan is to look at it as being made up of two parts: a strategic section and a tactical section. For a broad-gauge public relations program, both sections must be considered in fine detail. At the other extreme, a product publicity project may require only a tactical section, since the strategic considerations may be implicitly obvious to everyone involved.

Ideally, the strategic and tactical parts of a program are planned separately, on different levels of an organization's hierarchy. Strategic planning ideally is done on the top management level and tactical planning on the operational level. But in practice, the planning process is not so clear-cut and the distinctions between what is strategic and what is tactical may become blurred. Written plans usually reflect this. This means that the following methods and approaches probably cannot be applied universally or totally.

Strategic Considerations

Information of a more general nature such as guidance and direction from high-level executives makes up this part of a plan. The specific considerations involved are scope, purpose, procedures, resources, and priorities.

The scope of course is a statement of what the program will cover, and gives specific limitations if there are any.

Purpose includes the overall objective and theme of the program. The procedures spell out the methodology to be used in implementing the program, and the responsibilities of individuals or functions involved. They should include a means for evaluation and reporting of results, and for communication of information regarding the program.

The resources section is a statement of the manpower and money available to carry out the program. It should include the resources required for contingencies and "unproductive" activity, such as visiting and lunching with editors and writers to see what the opportunities are for supplying them with information. Paul B. Zucker, vice-president of Ruder and Finn, Inc., has stated that at least 25 percent of the available time for goal accomplishment should be left uncommitted to allow for unexpected contingencies. This "elbow room" or flexibility should be built into the planning, so that when the unexpected does occur it can be handled. Contingencies may come from either inside or outside an organization, and may be in the form of either problems or opportunities.

Priorities are often extremely important. Most programs are overly ambitious and often everything planned is not accomplished. When priorities are spelled out, it is possible to identify the important things and do them if the manpower and money cannot be stretched far enough to complete the entire program.

The following questions are often useful in helping to establish priorities.

- How good a match is there between what is desirable and what is possible?
- Is the vehicle for the message, the subject, newsworthy?
- Is the subject timely?
- What is the actual potential for helping to sell something or helping to build the stature of the organization?
- What resources are required to complete the job, and is the organization entitled to the amount of resources needed?
- Is information readily available?
- Are photos available or can they be taken using a minimum of time and money?
- Is the subject "photogenic" in the sense that photos of it, or concerning it, will be of use to publications?

- Is there anything that is particularly sensitive about the subject area either inside or outside the organization?
- Is the nature of the subject such that follow-up will be possible if questions are raised by press representatives, customers, or others?

Tactical Considerations

This part of the plan is concerned with operational considerations, specific subject matter, and the methods of accomplishing the individual tasks of the program. The items that make up this section are goals, audiences, subjects, tools and techniques, timing, and special resources.

The goals are the specific objectives tied to specific messages. The audiences are the market for information, and are made up of the publics to be reached and the media through which the information is distributed. The subjects of course are the specific products, technological areas, financial matters, and so on, that are the substantive part of the program. The tools and techniques are the particular devices, such as press releases, used to put out the information.

It is worthwhile to note that planning involving a particular objective and subject area may come this far in the planning process, only to be found to be unfeasible or not worth the effort. In this case, it can only be scrapped.

Timing should be considered from two viewpoints. The first involves production, and the second execution. In most cases, there are some critical milestone dates—such as delivery of a piece of equipment, completion of testing, an individual's presence at a particular place—which affect the production of publicity material. So it is necessary to know the critical milestone dates that can affect the preparation of material. The other viewpoint involves determination of the best time to accomplish a publicity project. This is of course linked to the goal. The reason for doing something and the time to do it should be considered together. Timing involves putting specific dates on some kind of schedule.

Special resources are manpower and money that may be needed over and above the normal allocation. For example, if a company that normally serves only a domestic market finds it necessary to carry out a publicity project overseas, extra resources have to be made available. Another example: A newsweekly magazine once wanted to take its own photo of a large, complicated diving system used for underwater work. The system was ashore between jobs. The cost of leasing a barge, working out the logistics, and bringing in personnel was determined to be $5000. This had not been planned in the publicity program, and the money had to be found elsewhere.

An interested executive had the funds transferred from a budget other than the normal publicity budget.

Example Plans

Two example plans are given below. They represent two extremes. The first is an abbreviated, completely capability-oriented plan. The second is a longer, hardware-oriented plan. Another contrast between the two is that the first plan is less formal and is in the form of a letter. The second is in a more formalized plan form. Both plans are taken from actual publicity programs, but names and numbers have been changed.

The first example is a letter to the director of a study group. The group is referred to here as TT which stands for "think tank." This letter illustrates that planning is a continual process. It gives the strategic part of the program, but also deals somewhat with the tactical. Most of the tactical is, however, left for future planning. The letter also shows that education is very definitely part of the publicity planning process in that a fairly long paragraph is devoted completely to an explanation of some publicity tools that appeared to be applicable to the group's situation and needs.

Dear John:

First of all, I'd like to thank you for your hospitality in our meeting on May 20. Your responsiveness and cooperation, and that of the TT professional staff, was encouraging.

Following are some of the highlights of our discussion, as I recall them. If I've misinterpreted anything, please correct me.

As a first step in getting the TT publicity efforts underway, you plan to put together an "annotated" list of subjects that I should know about and possibly focus upon.

We agreed upon a simple procedure to follow generally in getting signed articles written and published. The procedure is:

    1. TT staff members will provide extended outlines or synoptic write-ups of what the articles are to cover. The thing to keep in mind here is that these are actually to be article proposals.

    2. I'm to evaluate the article proposals, discuss them with the authors if necessary and present them to appropriate publications.

    3. I'm then to help the authors plan their articles and do whatever I can to assure that the articles will be published.

In addition to signed articles, we talked about the other types of material that we can generate to tell our story. First is the background type of information we supply to publications for use as the basis of staff-written articles. It can be in just about any form ranging from raw data to a piece of writing developed for another purpose (such as a presented paper) to a write-up generated especially for use in a magazine-written article. The use the publication makes of such background information varies widely. In some cases, I've seen it perform only as a device to capture the interest of an editor with the editor developing his own article from scratch. On the other hand, I've also seen cases where a publication has used the write-up we supplied almost word-for-word but under the byline of the editor. In the latter situation, the publications have always credited us satisfactorily within the articles.

The second type of material, other than the signed TT article, that we can generate is the news release. News releases for TT would probably take one of these two forms: the announcement, or the short, "popularized" version of a specialized but newsworthy subject.

I gathered from your comments that the objectives of our publicity activities are: (1) to identify TT as a leading study group with long experience and a highly capable staff, (2) show that the company, through TT, has the capability for and is actively engaged in systems and operational analysis which is directed at human betterment.

We talked about a couple of specific things that we can do in the near future. One is a news release that would briefly describe TT, using your move to a new building as the reason for distributing the release.

Another thing we could do is to show Dr. Smith's paper on arms deployment to one of the editors of *Defense Technology* to see if the magazine would be interested in doing an article based on it. Such an article would be written by one of the magazine's editors but I'm sure both Dr. Smith and TT would receive adequate credit in the article. We would of course have to time this so that there would be no conflict with the paper's publication in the journal.

I look forward to a productive association with you and the TT professional staff.

The second example is a publicity program for the fictitious John Doe Tool Company. In addition to illustrating a product-oriented program, it also demonstrates the point made above: that the planning process is not so neat or clear-cut in real life as in theory.

PUBLICITY PROGRAM

John Doe Tool Company

Scope

This program covers a time period of one year and applies only to the company's pump line. A management decision has been made to limit the program to the use of press releases and signed articles.

Purpose

The guiding purpose of the program is to support marketing efforts. Wherever possible, the reliability of the products and the depth of engineering experience in the field should be emphasized.

Specific Objectives

1. Improve JDT's identification and recognition in the utility industry.
2. Identify new markets where JDT can exploit its capabilities.
3. Stimulate customer inquiries for the pump line.

Primary Audiences

1. Electric utilities and their suppliers.
2. Nuclear systems designers and producers.

Tools and Techniques

1. Use by-lined technical articles on methods and equipment to show by implication the company's competence and ability. These articles should be written by engineers, management, or administrators for business and technical magazines.

2. Use news releases to provide product information and to show competence, emphasis on reliability and quality control, and relatively low cost for high-quality work. News releases may take the form of stories about developments, achievements, contract awards, deliveries, new equipment or facilities, progress reports, announcement of new products, or personnel changes.

3. Use application articles to show customer satisfaction, and the applicability and versatility of products or services supplied to a customer at his location. These should be written by engineers involved in the project; it is often possible and useful to have an article coauthored by a JDT man and one of the customer's engineers.

4. Use visits to JDT by key editors—an economical and successful technique for obtaining editorial space in important magazines. This technique can be used to implement nearly every objective. The advantages are:

- JDT management has the best opportunity it will ever have to suggest and offer article subjects directly to the editors—such article subjects, if an article results, can be very valuable.
- Less time is spent by JDT in producing and placing articles or news releases. Arrangements can be made directly with the editor to supply information, or an agreement can be reached on the exact content of a signed article.
- A write-up on a subject by an editor in one of the business or technical publications has more believability than a comparable article based on one of our news releases.
- Since editors necessarily have a great deal of knowledge in their field, plus the benefit of an overall view of the field, and since interviews are a two-way exchange, the visits can be a valuable source of intelligence.

Recommended Procedure

Planning the program:

1. Establish an operating plan.
2. Assign an individual as publicity coordinator with the responsibility for coordinating news release information and the writing of articles.
3. Prepare a definite program of news releases and article subjects listing the source or author and a completion date for each project. Every project on the program should specifically support one or more of the publicity objectives.

Implementing the program:

1. The publicity group and the JDT publicity coordinator then work with authors and those responsible for supplying news release information so that each project is completed on schedule.
2. News release preparation.

Responsibility	Steps
JDT	Coordinator collects news release information
JDT and publicity group	Obtain photos
JDT	Preliminary approval of information by JDT by the coordinator
Publicity group	Prepare release in appropriate form
Publicity group	Obtain company approvals on final draft of release
JDT	Obtain customer approvals when required
Publicity group	Coordinate release date with advertising and public relations
Publicity group	Distribute release to the press and internal activities

3. Article preparation.

Responsibility	Steps
JDT author and publicity group	Prepare outline
JDT coordinator	Obtain preliminary approval of outline from department manager
Publicity group	Submit outline to appropriate publication(s) to obtain a commitment from an editor to publish the article
JDT author	Write article and prepare illustrations (with assistance from the publicity group when requested)
Publicity group	Obtain corporate approval for publication
JDT	Obtain customer approval when required
Publicity group	Keep advertising and public relations departments informed on project
Publicity group	Handle all publication details with publications, notify JDT of acceptance and publication, provide copies of published article, supply reprints on order

Updating the Program

At intervals of three months, update the program at a planning meeting; drop inactive projects and add appropriate new projects.

Program Report

At intervals of six months, the publicity group will prepare a report evaluating progress and summarizing results.

Media

Primary Publications

Utility	Nuclear	Materials
Electrical World	*Nucleonics, Nucleonics News*	*Materials in Design Engineering*
Power	*Atomics*	*Metal Progress*
Electric Light & Power	ANS publications	*Steel*
Power Engineering	(*Nuclear News, Nuclear Engineering*)	*Iron Age*
Public Power		

Secondary Publications

Utility	Industrial	Scientific
Electrical West	*Business Week*	*International Science &*
		Technology
Electrical South	*Dun's Review*	*Industrial Research*
	Factory	*Research/Development*
	Mill & Factory	
	Plant Engineering	
	Automation	
	Southern Power & Industry	

Design Engineering	Other
Electrical Engineering	*Purchasing*
Electro-Technology	*Aviation Week*
Control Engineering	*Missiles & Rockets*
Machine Design	*Space Aeronautics*
Design News	*Chemical Engineering*
Product Engineering	
Mechanical Engineering	

(continued on page 91)

REFERENCES

George Black, *Planned Industrial Publicity*, Putnam Publishing Company, Chicago, Ill., 1952.

Raymond Simon, Ed., *Perspective in Public Relations*, University of Oklahoma Press, Norman, Okla., 1966.

B. W. Hoyle, *Information Services in Public Welfare Agencies*, WA Publication 19, Welfare Administration, U.S. Department of Heatlh, Education and Welfare, U.S. Government Printing Office, Washington, D.C., 1960.

Subject	Objective	Publicity Projects
Largest pumped storage water pump ever built	Show engineering and manufacturing experience and ability	1. News release—contract announcement 2. News release—construction underway of largest pumped storage water pump ever built 3. Article—how JDT overcame the problems in designing and building the largest pumped storage water pump ever produced 4. News release—delivery and installation story
Controlled-leakage pump	Illustrate unequaled engineering capability. Tell customers of availability of radically new and economical type of pump	1. News release—announcement of development 2. Article—features of the new JDT controlled-leakage pump
Automatic test equipment for large pumps	Show that JDT is ready and able to meet customer's needs	1. News release—announcement of final development of equipment 2. Article—how to test canned motor pumps through use of specially designed equipment
Dynamic shock analysis	Illustrate quality control consciousness and ingenuity in application of new concepts	1. News release—announcement of perfection of dynamic shock analysis technique 2. Article—testing by dynamic shock analysis
New process in welding large pump flanges	Illustrate ability to put new concepts to use, show manufacturing capability	Article—for metalworking magazine
New data processing system	Show emphasis on quality control and foresight of JDT	News release and article—new data processing system helps JDT keep quality up, cost down
Clean room with 30-ton crane	Illustrate sophistication of facilities, emphasis on quality control, and manufacturing capability	News release—clean room with 30-ton crane insures reliability of nuclear plant equipment.
Omnimill installation	Illustrate modernness of facilities and exceptional manufacturing capability	News release—JDT keeps its modern facility up-to-date with latest equipment.

8

IMPLEMENTATION AND EVALUATION OF PUBLICITY PLANS

This chapter is a transition and an introduction. It bridges a gap between the largely abstract exercise of planning and the actual work. It also introduces the next unit of the book, which deals with the forms of publicity information and the methods used in doing the industrial publicity job.

Implementation is the carrying out, accomplishment, fulfillment, or execution of an objective or a plan. Obviously, it is not the only—or maybe even not the best—word for the process.

MANPOWER AND SUPPORT

There is a variety of ways to do publicity work. These can be broken down into three categories:

- Fully staffed in-house publicity group that does the entire job.
- Small in-house group (often one individual) that uses the talents and resources available elsewhere in the organization.
- In-house publicity director (who often has other responsibilities and performs this function on a part-time basis) supported by outside services.

Several things influence the method used in doing the publicity job. Foremost among them are company factors such as size, type of management, type of employees and their attitudes, type of products, internal costs, and budgeting methods. Other factors are the size and type of marketplace in which the company does its business, and the media that serve the marketplace.

There is little agreement on the question of whether it is better to buy outside services or to staff up to handle publicity internally. However, there are some considerations that apply in many cases. One is general acceptance of the rule of thumb that says companies with sales in the $5 to $10 million per year range probably do not have the resources to do the job internally; and companies with sales over $25 million per year should be able to do a reasonably effective job themselves. But even in the case in which a company can justify an internal publicity operation, outside services will probably be needed somewhere along the line because of work load peaks and special problems. It is probably safe to say that a combination of the internal and external approaches is best in most cases.

In comparing the cost of external versus internal service, one thing that is sometimes overlooked is the effect of indirect costs on the internal operation. In addition to the direct costs of salary and operating expenses, costs such as fringe benefits, vacations and sick leaves, telephone service, and working space must also be considered. Indirect costs can amount to as much as direct costs.

Fully Staffed Publicity Group

Large companies or organizations usually use this approach. They generally have a group of publicity managers and experts in the corporate staff organization that serves the divisions or departments. Sometimes the lower echelons have publicity people, or people who perform the publicity function, in addition to the staff group. These publicity groups use outside help usually only when they have an overload or when it is clearly less expensive. For example, if an east coast company wants to obtain a case history story on the west coast, it may be less expensive to hire a west coast writer or agency to do the job than to send a staff man out. Smaller companies generally do not have the resources to have an in-house publicity group. Also, they might not have enough publicity to be done to justify a group.

Small Internally Supported Group

Small- and medium-sized companies or organizations often take the approach of giving a small group (sometimes just an individual full-time and even only part-time) responsibility for a publicity program. In most cases these groups or individuals do not have the budget to spend much on outside services. In these cases, they use manpower and resources elsewhere in the organization to do the job. This means that the publicity director must persuade the managers of other functions such as marketing and engineering that it is necessary for them to support the publicity effort with manpower, money, or both. And with all the demands for resources made upon these managers, they are difficult to convince. Often this approach is not the most effective use of everyone's time, and it is probably used more often than it should be. Also, it often bogs down completely, as illustrated by the following example.

The case involved a materials department headed by a highly competent materials engineer with an international reputation. In addition to technical competence, however, he had a very good grasp of business and management ideas and practices. He agreed fully on the importance of a strong publicity program. However, he and the several engineers and technicians working for him were putting in long hours in lab work and were spending a great deal of their own time working on reports on the lab work and on proposals for contracts, both essential to the profitability of the department. Progress reports were overdue, a few key projects were behind schedule, and a technical paper the manager had committed himself to write was late. He agreed in principle, but felt unable to do anything to support the publicity effort.

Such instances are not rarities. And in some organizations, they are the single largest block to an effective publicity program. What often happens in such instances is that the engineering group, or whatever kind of group it happens to be, promises to support a publicity program, with no real ability to follow through. They just want the publicity director out of their hair.

Besides inefficiencies such as lip-service support, the use of "contributed" resources within the organization has another disadvantage. It diffuses both responsibility and authority. And "What is everybody's business is nobody's business."

Despite the disadvantages of this approach, in many cases the resources are simply not available to do the job any other way. There are some things that can be done to alleviate the problem. They are:

- Use a "direct mail" approach.
- Enlist suppliers, customers, and distributors in a cooperative publicity program.

The so-called direct mail approach can make use of questionnaires, motivational material, and incentives.

One company used a combination of a questionnaire and an incentive. It gave a cash award of $25 for every case history questionnaire its field salesmen filled out and sent in. The case history information was used in some cases for advertising and in others for publicity.

Enlisting the aid of a supplier or other outside "volunteer" organization should be done by the individual who is its primary contact. In the case of a supplier, this would be a purchasing agent; for a customer, a salesman; for a distributor, a marketing director or manager. These individuals know the companies or groups they deal with and are able to judge whether or not they will be receptive to a cooperative program.

Another possible source of help is a technical writing group. Many companies, even small ones, especially those that do government work, have such groups. They work on all kinds of manuals, handbooks, and other material often referred to by the general term "documentation." The material is usually instructive in nature. Its most common form is military equipment documentation—operation, maintenance, and repair manuals. There are, however, countless other forms.

Some technical writers know, or can learn, enough about publicity to produce useful press releases and articles. The caveat here is that most technical writers do not write anything original. They simply make more understandable and readable information they have been given. And this level of "writing" ability may in fact be all that is required in certain cases. However, if any interpretation or generalizing is required in the writing, most technical writers will be at a loss. They usually cannot shift their specialized attitude enough to do an adequate job.

In addition to their writing potential, technical writers can also be useful in illustrating material. They are responsible for illustrations in the manuals and other documentation they produce, and work very closely with illustrators and photographers. But here again, their specialized viewpoint may be more of a hindrance than a help.

External Support

The types of external support available are individual producers, consultants, and agencies. Individual producers can include writers, photographers, or a combination of the two known as photojournalists. Individual producers are used to write material and illustrate news releases and articles that support some objective of a publicity plan. Their role has nothing to do with planning or counseling.

Consultants on the other hand usually do nothing *but* counsel. (High-caliber public relations consultants are known as PR counsels.) In some cases, their advice is in the area of organizing to do a publicity job; in other cases, it involves publicity planning as well. Some individuals who call themselves consultants go beyond the giving of advice and also do the work of carrying out a plan. In this capacity, they function as a one-man agency.

Agencies are hired either on a retainer basis or as needed to carry out a specific program or solve a specific problem.

The type of external support the company needs depends largely on its in-house capability and the state of its business. Companies needing external publicity support can be categorized as:

- Small company beginning or expanding its publicity effort.
- Small or large company needing external support for a limited time.
- Large company that likes to keep staff activities lean and prefers to buy service outside rather than enlarging its publicity unit.
- Large company that needs external support to help keep its publicity people objective and outward-looking instead of becoming primarily concerned with internal affairs.

When a small company just getting into publicity, or expanding its publicity effort, has a full-time publicity director with considerable experience, it will probably use individual producers and agencies. If a small company has a part-time director for this activity, or one who has little experience in the publicity field, the company may want to use both a consultant and an agency. In the latter case, the consultant either can be used initially to organize the publicity activity and then step out of the picture, or can stay on to supervise the agency's activities.

Agencies and individual producers are used by small and large companies that need external support for a limited time to carry out a special project or to help solve a particular short-range problem. They are also used by large companies that need external support on a continuing basis.

Consultants and agencies are used in the fourth case, where a large company feels it needs outside eyes to look at its activities to keep its attitudes relevant to the needs and opportunities among its publics.

Consultants and individual producers usually work on the basis of a letter or memorandum of understanding rather than a formal written contract. Many agencies do also, but contracts are not uncommon.

There are far more agencies than consultants and individual producers. Small agencies, and consultants and individual producers, are usually highly specialized. This is one of their strengths.

The way to locate outside support is to ask professionals in other companies, talk to editors, and talk to as many potential contributors as possible.

Some of the key questions in determining the type of external support needed are:

- Is the support required to be of a counseling nature, or will actual publicity work be needed? If it is counseling, a consultant is probably called for. If work is to be performed, an agency or an individual producer is in order.

- What are the short- and long-term objectives? Short-term objectives usually imply a one-shot or limited publicity project. In such a situation an agency or an individual producer is usually used. In the case of long-term objectives, a consultant may be needed to map out the strategy, and an agency or individual contributor to carry out the plans.
- What is the size of the job to be done? In the case of a very extensive program, a large agency is often used because it has the necessary resources.
- What is the extent of the funds available? If a very small amount of money is available, an individual producer may be the only acceptable alternative. Many agencies consider an account of less than $10,000 a year unprofitable and will not accept it. Consultants are usually more expensive than individual producers, but the quality of the publicity program is much higher.
- How much in-house expertise is available? As indicated above, if the publicity director runs a one-man shop and has little experience in the field, he may need the advice of a consultant to start him down the right path.

Important to the effectiveness of any type of external support is the matter of accountability versus authority. If agencies or individuals are to be held accountable to a high degree, they should also have a lot of authority delegated to them by the client. They should be free to make commitments and decisions they feel are necessary to carry out their responsibilities and meet the expectations of the client.

Consultants

The least used, but not necessarily the least valuable, type of external support is the consultant. The qualifications of a publicity consultant are much the same as for other types of consultants, He should have broad experience, proven performance, and an in-depth understanding of the way organizations work. He must be a problem solver, and he must always put the client first.

Before bringing in a consultant, it is necessary to make sure that the key people in the company will cooperate and be receptive. It is also necessary to define carefully the purpose or the problem to which the consultant will apply his expertise.

The next step is to locate a consultant and work out with him the scope of his task. In conjunction with this, the fee should be negotiated. This may run from $100 to $250 per day.

Once the consultant is brought in, he should be given all the facts. It is essential to be completely candid, even to the extent of admitting the fears and prejudices of key individuals.

Individual Producers

Individual producers are individuals in the sense that they usually work alone. They are sometimes members of a group of associated writers or photographers, they may be employed by concerns that provide such services, and in some cases they are free lancers.

The majority of individual producers are generalists in terms of knowledge and experience. They know quite a bit about a lot of different kinds of things. Usually, they are ex-journalists or ex-photojournalists. Other individual producers have specialized knowledge and experience. Many are technically trained, and some are former editors of trade and technical publications. Some photographers come from specialized areas such as industrial photography.

Individual producers may charge for their services on a flat fee or a time basis. On a time basis, writers usually charge by the hour for time spent in researching and writing. Photographers usually charge by the day. Whether they are on a time or flat fee basis, writers and photographers always bill expenses connected with the job to their clients at cost.

Many companies prefer writers to work for a fixed price, so they know exactly how much a job will cost. This is often more expensive than the time basis, because writers usually pad a fixed-fee quotation. It is not because they are dishonest, but simply because they are not willing to risk losing money. Every writer knows from experience that some jobs take more time than expected. So he inflates the price to make up for the unprofitable jobs.

Writers and photographers calculate their fees by adding together a salary, overhead costs, and reasonable profit, and then dividing that figure by the number of working hours in whatever time frame they have selected.

It is probably safe to say that more individual producers, both generalists and specialists, work on case histories than on any other type of story.

The idea that the case history is one of the more useful tools in the publicity arsenal is developed in Chapter 9.

Individual producers are in most cases the most "cost-effective" method of having case history material prepared. Those that have become known as effective producers at reasonable cost have developed clienteles. A pattern that has evolved is that such producers make swings to various parts of the country to carry out specific assignments. By informing their clientele that they are making a particular trip, they often obtain additional assignments. By combining such assignments, they can spread the expenses around among several clients. Some have done this so successfully that they have developed a flat rate for jobs just about anywhere in the country.

The other more-or-less common way outside writers are used is for ghost writing, mostly speeches and signed articles. Busy executives do not always have the time to write things themselves, so they or someone on their staff turns these chores over to someone else. The writer is told in general terms what the executive wants to say. He then talks to staff members and experts, and may even visit a plant or other location to get a feeling for the atmosphere. The mark of a good ghost is the amount of work he puts into research before even outlining what is to be written. This of course takes a lot of time, and there may be expenses involved. Sometimes, those who are responsible for buying the writing services are surprised at the cost, especially if they have never done anything similar before.

Outside individual producers of course can be used to produce all the other forms of industrial publicity in addition to case histories and ghost-written material. Covered in detail in Chapters 9 and 10, these forms of industrial publicity include various types of press releases, unsigned exclusive material, signed exclusive articles, speeches, papers, and material for company publications.

Agencies

Agencies come in all sizes and have all kinds of different characteristics and expertise. The first major problem in shopping for an agency is matching an agency's capabilities with the needs and characteristics of the organization. For example, it is possible that an agency performs brilliantly in creative work, but that the account executive or manager cannot communicate with his counterpart in the company. Another agency might have less creative power, but has an account executive who works well with the client.

Most agencies are either advertising or public relations agencies. Some large ones do both. With the exception of financial public relations, what is called public relations by agencies that operate in the public sector is usually industrial publicity.

Evaluating agencies is a highly subjective matter. Some of the things that can be used in an agency evaluation are:

- Accomplishments. These reveal a lot about the agency's creative abilities and the kinds of things they are good at. The other side of that coin is that failures can also show a lot about the agency.
- People. An investigation of the abilities, attitudes, and experience of management, account men, and creative individuals is also revealing.

It helps provide a picture of an agency's total talent, its stability and reliability, and its integrity, and gives an indication of the compatability of the agency and the company.

- Cost. Agencies usually charge on a time basis for publicity services. Everyone in an agency is required to keep daily records of how much time is spent working for each account. These accounts are then billed monthly for the total amount of time spent on them. If an agency is on a retainer, it provides service on an agreed-upon basis or on demand up to the value of the retainer. If additional service is required, a fee is then negotiated over and above the retainer.
- Physical factors. The location of the agency is a consideration. It should be easy for agency people to reach the company, and vice versa. Another consideration is the location of other offices of the agency, if any, which can be called upon if necessary. If, for example, there is a possibility of needing services overseas, it might be a good idea to try to find an agency with overseas offices. The size of the agency is another element—which can be either positive or negative.

It is important to recognize that there can be a difference between real and apparent competence in evaluating support of any kind. For example, for agencies, a fact of life is making presentations to clients or prospective clients. They put a lot of effort into these presentations, and justifiably so because they are the primary means of communicating their abilities. Individual producers usually engage in a certain amount of salesmanship, for obvious reasons. No one wants to hire an inarticulate person. The point of all this is that salesmanship is sometimes confused with product quality.

The vast majority of agencies are of course ethical, and they do not try to sell their clients worthless services. But it is useful to remember that agencies, just like companies, must make a profit to stay in business. That does not mean that they are unscrupulous, but they practice entrepreneurship in looking for opportunities to increase their billings.

A final caveat: Free or nonprofit publicity services provided by advertising agencies are often inferior. This approach should generally be avoided.

INFORMATION

The forms of publicity information are described in some detail in Chapters 9 and 10, and the means of implementation are to a large extent covered in the descriptions. However, some factors not covered there affect implementation. These factors are related to the nature of the organization and to the publicity plans.

Organization Influence

The type of organization is a major influence. At one extreme is the small, limited-product-line unit which has high-volume production of relatively simple and competitive products. Such a unit may be a company, or it may be the smallest unit with profit responsibility in a corporate structure. Publicity for such a unit may be handled independently of the rest of the organization, even if it is part of a corporate structure.

The publicity program for such a small unit is usually very specific and highly focused. It is most often completely marketing oriented, as opposed to supporting public relations objectives. It is aimed at very specific audiences—generally well-defined customer audiences—and uses specialized media.

The other extreme of organization type is the corporate unit in which publicity is handled by a corporate staff. This permits a lot of specialized ability to be applied to programs, but very often the corporate staff is not completely attuned to the needs and problems of the lesser units.

It is probably safe to say that in most large corporations the main responsibility of the corporate staff is public relations publicity as opposed to marketing support publicity. In cases in which the lesser units have responsibility for their own publicity activities to some degree or another, the corporate staff has the added responsibility for coordinating the publicity activities of the units so they do not work at cross purposes and get in each other's way.

Corporate programs are usually much more general in nature and aimed at larger and less specialized audiences. They are oriented toward the large circulation media, the general-interest magazines, newspapers, and the electronic media.

Most organizational units fall somewhere between the small, strictly limited unit and the corporate unit, so there is usually an element of both marketing and public relations support in a real-world program.

Whatever the type of program, it must at some point be translated into action. This is where the tools and techniques covered in the next two chapters come in.

Information Forms and Methods

Briefly, the forms of information used fall in two broad categories: syndicated and exclusive information. Syndicated material is sent to many publications at the same time. Exclusive information is given to a single publication. Syndicated material is most commonly in the form of a press release. Exclusive material is usually in the form of an article which is substantially longer than a press release and may or may not be signed by someone. That is, someone's name appears under the title as a by-line.

Also, there are two broad categories of methods of putting information into the hands of editors and writers. These are indirect and direct means. When indirect means are used, information is passed along to recipients by mail, teletype, or telephone. In direct transfer of information, the recipient is given the information personally. This can take place on either an individual or collective basis. The individual basis may be through a visit to or from an editor; the collective through a briefing or a press conference.

PROBLEMS AND LIMITATIONS

Overcapacity

A major problem in industrial publicity is what *Fortune* magazine once referred to as "a kind of 'overcapacity' problem. Its [industry's] capabilities for spreading the message are immense. The trouble is that it's hard to find messages worth spreading; to a large and dispiriting extent, the p.r. output that lands on most businessmen's and editor's desks belongs in their wastebasket—and gets there within seconds of the landing."

Fortune's statement may not be completely accurate, but the point is valid. This is borne out by a comment made by Richard Koff, formerly managing editor of *Product Engineering* magazine. He said that the magazine receives about 15,000 press releases per year, but uses information from only 2000, about 13 percent of the total.

The reasons so few releases are used can be viewed in terms of an editor's interest. If the release is not of interest to an editor, he simply does not use it. The editor's interest is of course an extension of his readers' views.

If a release does not interest an editor, it is either poorly done or misdirected. The problem of producing press releases is dealt with in Chapter 9 and 12; the misdirection problem is considered in Chapter 9 in sections concerned with dissemination and placement.

It is usually possible to find an interesting angle in almost any subject area, but occasionally it is not. If the latter is the case, the project should be dropped from the plan as soon as it becomes apparent that it will be a waste of time.

Proprietary Information

Another consideration under the heading of problems and limitations is that of proprietary information. This falls into one of two categories, competitive information and information about patentable inventions.

Competitive information is of the company and trade secret type. It includes such things as market and financial data, and information about processes and product know-how.

Information about patentable inventions can be extremely valuable to a company. Patents give the company the right to the exclusive use of information on processes or devices. It can sell its patents, or license other companies to produce patented inventions. However a company handles its patents, they are usually worth a lot of money. Very often, a company goes to a lot of expense to develop an invention, and if it cannot be patented, competitors may get the benefit.

The patent problem in the United States is different from that in most other countries. In the United States, if information about a patentable invention is published, the company has a year to file for a patent. In most other countries, the company cannot obtain a patent after the date the information is published anywhere in the world. So if a company does business overseas, it is in their best interests to file for a patent before they disclose information by publication.

Even if a company is not doing overseas business and has no licensees overseas, it is a good idea not to disclose information on something that is patentable. The reason is that it may stimulate a competitor to file for a patent on the same thing. The first to file is in a better legal position in any patent dispute. The burden of proof is on the company that files second. Being on the defensive is always a disadvantage, especially in patent disputes.

A way to avoid the patent problem is of course to avoid premature disclosure of information on something that is patentable. The one that is in the best position to make a judgment as to what constitutes premature disclosure is the company's, or unit's, patent attorney. He should therefore have a chance to see information about new products or procedures in advance of disclosure. And since industrial publicity is concerned with new information, it should be one of the types of information the patent attorney is shown.

Sensitivity

Yet another item in the catalog of problems and limitations is a rather nebulous subject that might be called sensitivity. One form it takes is knowing what *not* to say as well as what *to* say. Saying the wrong thing can sometimes be worse than saying nothing.

Sometimes, publicity done for its own sake can amount to saying the wrong thing. Those responsible for putting out publicity often feel compelled, or are expected, to use numerous pieces of press information or clippings as a measure of their effectiveness. In many such instances, realistic planning and relevant objectives are given lip service, and the aim becomes the production of material whether it does any good or not. Given such a situation, the odds are that at some point a press release will go out or an article will be placed or some other action will be taken that results in bad press.

An example of a situation in which the wrong thing is said is the following hypothetical case:

The ABC company makes an electronic tube that produces a television picture in almost total darkness. The main use of the tube is in a television camera that is part of a night bombing system on a military airplane. But there are other uses, such as watching streets, parking lots, parks, and so on, at night, possibly for crime prevention. Now suppose that the publicity director has a press release on the remarkable performance of the television camera tube in the bombing system and, wonder of wonders, obtains approval from the military customer to distribute it. In making up a mailing list, he decides that the press release should be sent to municipal and law enforcement publications because the tube can be useful in night surveillance for crime prevention. But one of the national municipal publications he sends the release to has an editor who is violently antimilitary. The bombing system mentioned in the release so incenses the editor that in a fit of anger he dashes off an editorial about companies that build instruments of war and, to make matters even worse, try to exploit people in trouble using their ill-gotten technology.

Although such an extreme case of bad press is unlikely to happen, it illustrates the problem of wrong information or information in the wrong place. Ineffective or misdirected information is not the mark of a professional.

Another form of sensitivity is to be alert to the possibility of something unfavorable or even disastrous happening in the publicity process. This is illustrated by the following cases:

CASE 1

A publicity writer and his photographer were researching and taking pictures of an electrical system in a new plant. Their company had supplied the electrical system. One of the photos they wanted was of a bank of cabinets housing parts of the electrical system. When they arrived, they found one of the cabinet doors open. Although they did not know it, a technicial had opened the cabinet to make an adjustment. All such cabinets that have high-power components have interlocks to shut off the power in the cabinet to prevent injury if one of the cabinets opens or is opened. The technician had "cheated" the interlock in order to open and keep the door open so he could work on the circuits while the power was on. The writer innocently closed the cabinet, which activated the interlock, shutting off the power in the cabinet, which in turn automatically shut down an entire process line. This naturally caused a great amount of trouble and unnecessary expense. The writer and photographer were escorted from the plant, and it was a long time before representatives of any kind from their company were welcome there.

CASE 2

A major supplier of jet aircraft engines with great difficulty arranged to have five different military aircraft that used the company's engines fly in formation to take pictures for advertising and publicity purposes. One of the aircraft was an experimental supersonic bomber and was the main reason for the pictures. The company wanted to show a progression of aircraft culminating in the bomber. The aircraft all rendezvoused in the air as planned. They came from different places, and most of them had legitimate reasons to be flying, such as test runs. They flew in formation, also as planned, and filming was begun from a nonmilitary plane provided by the company. Forty-one minutes after the formation flight began, the fighter flying at the bomber's right wing drifted into the big plane's wing and they both crashed. The pilot of the fighter and the copilot of the bomber did not eject and were killed. The terrible waste of human lives was bad enough, but there were other consequences. The careers of several Air Force officers were damaged because they had not followed proper procedures in obtaining approval for the flight. And the company earned one of the worst black eyes in industrial history, with concomitant distrust and loss of prestige.

The second case is of course an extreme example which hopefully will never be duplicated. Nevertheless, both cases illustrate the idea that it is necessary to assess the risk of something unexpected happening and what the probable consequences might be. If lives are at stake, projects such as the filming of an aircraft formation should not be undertaken. This also holds true if there is a possibility of expensive equipment being damaged or destroyed. Projects of lesser risk must be individually assessed.

Security and Contractual Requirements

Security requirements are another type of limitation. These can relate to company security, proprietary information, or government restrictions on information. For example, a part of every contract from the Department of Defense is a document designated form DD-254. This has a block in which a statement is entered indicating how information related to the work covered by the contract is to be handled. (See Figure 8-1.) Usually it says something like: "All information relating to work done under this contract must be

DEPARTMENT OF DEFENSE

CONTRACT SECURITY CLASSIFICATION SPECIFICATION

(Complete classified items by separate correspondence)

1. THE REQUIREMENTS OF THE DOD INDUSTRIAL SECURITY MANUAL APPLY TO PERFORMANCE OF THIS CONTRACT.

FACILITY SECURITY CLEARANCE REQUIRED FOR CONTRACT PERFORMANCE OR FOR ACCESS TO CLASSIFIED INFORMATION IS _____

4. THIS SPECIFICATION IS: *(See note below)*

a. ORIGINAL

b. REVISED *(Supersedes all previous specifications)*

c. FINAL

DATED

2.

	3. CONTRACT NUMBER OR OTHER IDENTIFICATION NUMBER *(Prime contracts must be shown for all subcontracts)*	DATE TO BE COMPLETED *(Estimated)*
THIS SPECIFICATION IS FOR:		
a. PRIME CONTRACT	*a.* PRIME	
b. SUBCONTRACT *(Use Item 8 to identify further subcontracting)*	*b.* FIRST TIER SUBCONTRACT	
c. INVITATION TO BID OR REQUEST FOR PROPOSAL	*c.* INVITATION FOR BID, REQUEST FOR PROPOSAL, OR REQUEST FOR QUOTE	

5. IF THIS IS A FOLLOW-ON CONTRACT, ENTER PRECEDING CONTRACT NUMBER AND DATE COMPLETED ☐ DOES NOT APPLY

CONTRACT NUMBER	DATE COMPLETED

6a. NAME AND ADDRESS OF PRIME CONTRACTOR *(Include ZIP Code)*

b. NAME AND ADDRESS OF COGNIZANT SECURITY OFFICE *(Include ZIP Code)*

7a. NAME AND ADDRESS OF FIRST TIER SUBCONTRACTOR *(If applicable)(Include ZIP Code)*

b. NAME AND ADDRESS OF COGNIZANT SECURITY OFFICE *(Include ZIP Code)*

8. SUBCONTRACTING BEYOND FIRST TIER *(as appropriate)*

(Use Item 8 to identify further subcontracting)

b. CONTRACT PRESCRIBES SECURITY REQUIREMENTS WHICH ARE ADDITIONAL TO THOSE PRESCRIBED IN DD FORM 441 AND THE IISM ☐ YES ☐ NO

REMARKS

10. CONTRACT PERFORMANCE WILL REQUIRE	YES	NO
GRAPHIC ARTS SERVICES		
ACCESS TO CONTROLLED AREAS OR CLASSIFIED INFORMATION ONLY		
MANUFACTURE OF CLASSIFIED HARDWARE		
GENERATION, RECEIPT, OR CUSTODY OF CLASSIFIED DOCUMENTS OR OTHER MATERIAL		
ACCESS TO RESTRICTED DATA		
ACCESS TO CRYPTOGRAPHIC INFORMATION		
ACCESS TO COMMUNICATION ANALYSIS INFORMATION		
DEFENSE DOCUMENTATION CENTER OR DEFENSE INFORMATION ANALYSIS CENTER SERVICES MAY BE REQUESTED (If yes, see paragraph T, app I, Industrial Security Manual.)		

11. REFER ALL QUESTIONS PERTAINING TO CONTRACT SECURITY CLASSIFICATION SPECIFICATION TO THE OFFICIAL NAMED BELOW (NORMALLY, thru ACO) (Item 14b); EMERGENCY, direct with written record of inquiry and response to ACO) (thru prime contractor for subcontracts)

a. PROGRAM/PROJECT MANAGER OR ACTIVITY (Name, Title, and Organization)

b. ADDRESS, TELEPHONE NUMBER AND OFFICE SYMBOL (Include ZIP Code)

NOTE: Original Specification (Item 4a) is authority for contractors to mark classified information. Revised and Final Specifications (Items 4b and c) are authority for contractors to remark the regraded classified information. Such actions by contractors shall be taken in accordance with the provisions of the industrial Security Manual.

DD FORM 1 APR 71 **254**   REPLACES EDITION OF 1 JUL 67, WHICH MAY BE USED.   PAGE 1 OF _____ PAGES

Figure 8-1. Page 1, Form DD-254.

12.

INFORMATION PERTAINING TO CLASSIFIED CONTRACTS OR PROJECTS, EVEN THOUGH SUCH INFORMATION IS CONSIDERED UNCLASSIFIED, SHALL NOT BE RELEASED FOR PUBLIC DISSEMINATION EXCEPT AS PROVIDED BY THE INDUSTRIAL SECURITY MANUAL(paragraph 5n and Appendix IX).

PROPOSED PUBLIC RELEASES SHALL BE SUBMITTED FOR APPROVAL PRIOR TO RELEASE ☐ DIRECT ☐ THROUGH (Specify)

TO THE DIRECTORATE FOR SECURITY REVIEW, OFFICE OF THE ASSISTANT SECRETARY OF DEFENSE (Public Affairs)* FOR REVIEW IN ACCORDANCE WITH PARAGRAPH 5n OF THE INDUSTRIAL SECURITY MANUAL.

*In the case of non-DoD user agencies, see footnote, paragraph 5n, Industrial Security Manual.

13. SECURITY CLASSIFICATION SPECIFICATIONS FOR THIS CONTRACT ARE SET FORTH BELOW (Check which are applicable):

☐ DD FORM 254C ATTACHED (hereby made a part of this specification).

☐ DOCUMENT(S) LISTED BELOW (hereby made part of this specification).

☐ AS STATED BELOW

CONTRACT SECURITY CLASSIFICATION SPECIFICATIONS FOR SUBCONTRACTS ISSUING FROM THIS CONTRACT WILL BE APPROVED BY THE OFFICIAL NAMED IN ITEM 14b BELOW.

REQUIRED DISTRIBUTION:

☐ PRIME CONTRACTOR *(Item 6a)*

☐ COGNIZANT SECURITY OFFICE *(Item 6b)*

☐ ADMINISTRATIVE CONTRACTING OFFICE *(Item 14b)*

☐ MATERIAL INSPECTOR

☐ SUBCONTRACTOR *(Item 7a)*

☐ COGNIZANT SECURITY OFFICE *(Item 7b)*

ADDITIONAL DISTRIBUTION:

☐ ☐

14. THIS CONTRACT SECURITY CLASSIFICATION SPECIFICATION AND ATTACHMENTS REFERENCED HEREIN, APPROVED BY THE USER AGENCY CONTRACTING OFFICER OR HIS REPRESENTATIVE NAMED BELOW:

SIGNATURE

TYPED NAME AND TITLE OF APPROVING OFFICIAL

a. APPROVING OFFICIAL'S ACTIVITY AND ADDRESS *(Include ZIP Code)*

b. NAME AND ADDRESS OF ADMINISTRATIVE CONTRACTING OFFICE *(Include ZIP Code)*

PAGE 2 OF _____ PAGES

Figure 8-2. Page 2, Form DD-254.

cleared by the contracting officer for open publication." Most other types of government contracts and commercial contracts have some provision in them for approval of information related to the contract. So it is necessary to be sure what the contractual obligations are before even beginning a publicity project.

Even though a contract may not require formal approval of information by the customer, it is frequently a good idea to inform him about a publicity project on work covered by his contract. It may even be advantageous to let him see information as a matter of courtesy and to maintain good customer relations.

Working with Executives and Experts

Yet another problems and limitations area is that of working with people in the company. The two main categories are executives, and experts and specialists.

Top executives are by definition more-or-less good at company politics. They are of course usually very capable people to begin with, but as a general statement they are also very adept at company politics. The publicity director usually is, or should be, in a privileged position with top management. Consequently, it is often difficult for him to not become entangled in company politics. He should, however, make a strong attempt to stay aloof from such political activity unless he is in line for a top management slot himself. The reason is that he can rarely win at that game. So he should try to stick to business.

Top-management men often have a reasonably good understanding of what publicity is and what it can do, because they see the operation of a company from an overall viewpoint. Since middle managers have a narrower view, they can create problems for the publicity director. A common way in which this is done is to exert pressure through budgetary controls and to withhold cooperation. He may have to resort to persuasion or, in some cases, arm twisting—which often amounts to playing company politics—to obtain the cooperation of lower-echelon managers on plans and procedures.

There also are special problems in working with experts and specialists. The majority of these individuals in practice turn out to be engineers. The main reason for the problems is that the experts often do not understand publicity and consider it suspect. Frequently they do not fully trust people involved in publicity. And that goes for advertising people too.

Another reason for the problems is that experts can be difficult to work with. Some are naturally uncommunicative and uncooperative, some cannot get their minds off their work, and some are just prima donnas.

Difficulties in working with experts sometimes come from their not being involved in publicity planning.

A good set of suggestions for working with experts was given by Michael K. Bonner in an article in the August 1958 issue of *Industrial Marketing* magazine. An editor's prefatory comment said, "Here are 18 'Do's' and 'Don'ts' suggested by author Bonner . . . to keep in mind when working with engineers. While these 'Do's' and 'Don'ts' apply specifically to publicity people concerned with feature articles in technical magazines, the approach is the same for any other kind of information activity."

Here are Bonners 'do's" and "don'ts":

1. *Do* plan the content and approach of the article *with* the engineer, not *for* him—he'll resent a self-made genius.

2. *Don't* appear on the scene just because you feel like it—make an appointment that is convenient for him.

3. *Do* let him know early in the planning what the technical levels of the magazine audience will be and what its range of interests is.

4. *Don't* rush him—let him set the pace of the meeting.

5. *Do* gain his respect by what you do, not what you claim to know about his field. Be careful about implying knowledge in his area (even though you may be an engineer); he'll be happy with your understanding alone.

6. *Don't* be afraid to ask questions or request elaboration. Errors in your text that are ridiculous to him can thus be avoided—and, anyway, there's nothing most engineers enjoy more than explaining what they are doing.

7. *Do* tell him about the operation of magazines behind the scenes—so that he understands why his work will be edited, why many months may pass before publication, why there may be types in the published article.

8. *Don't* ever ask him to do anything that he might consider is really your job—like library research.

9. *Do* be willing to lose the point on details in order to win his enthusiastic participation.

10. *Don't* bristle when he corrects your English or changes phraseology. Remember, his name (not yours) is on it—and you could be wrong.

11. *Do* inform him well in advance on deadline dates for his contributions, and make your inevitable reminders to him as pleasant as possible.

12. *Don't* ignore his opinion of magazines he reads regularly—he often knows the readers' point of view better than you.

13. *Do* introduce him, whenever possible, to editors so that he feels part of the program—don't be a middleman.

14. *Don't* waste his time—it's tough enough for him to find time for article work on the job or at home.

15. *Do* be certain that the author has OK'd the final version of the article exactly as it will be submitted to the editor.

16. *Don't* keep him in the dark on progress after his part is done. Tell him—as soon as you know—the editor's reactions and the publication dates.

17. *Do* remain in the background when bouquets are passed out (but take your share of any brickbats). He's the author; your job is only in transmission.

18. *Don't* give his suggestions on future projects a polite nod and no action. If followed up, keep him informed. If not, explain why.

EVALUATION

It may be argued that evaluation is not a subcategory under implementation, but a subject in itself. Even if this is the case, evaluation is very closely related to implementation and provides the feedback necessary to see if results are being obtained and if the plans continue to be meaningful.

Results Measurement

In industry, evaluation is usually thought of in terms of measuring something. The effectiveness of publicity is difficult to measure. This problem is very much like the difficulty of measuring the effectiveness of advertising. The most common gauge of publicity results is the volume of clippings generated by a press release, or the length of a feature article. But this does not indicate that anyone read the material or, if they did, whether the information had the desired effect.

It is especially hard to measure the effectiveness of image-building or capability publicity. Here, the only worthwhile way to tell if anything has been accomplished is to survey the attitudes of a specific public before and after a publicity campaign. Because of the cost and the time involved, this is practical only where there is a massive and continuing problem. An example might be the kind of ingrown awe of nuclear power that most people have. This is definitely a problem for electric utilities and their suppliers all over the world. On the one hand, nuclear power is considered in many instances the best, most economic way of dealing with the need for more power. On the other hand, there is a lot of opposition, some very powerful, to this energy source.

For relatively minor problems, more "routine" objectives, and small companies, surveys are often not practical. A workable alternative is to evaluate not the results but the performance of the program. The idea behind this is that a program carried out the way it should be generally achieves the desired results. The job must be done professionally by knowledgeable and thorough people. They will formulate meaningful objectives, at the right audience, and use the appropriate media. Their strategy is coherent and their tactics are workable. The material they generate is well done and appropriate. Information being published is as effective, or more so, than what competitors are doing. Spot checks with the media can be used to obtain further insight into performance.

So results at the image-building and capability publicity end of the spectrum are very difficult to measure. At the other end of the spectrum is product publicity, and its results lend themselves more readily to measurement. And since more product publicity is generated than any other type, it may be useful to explore its evaluation in some depth.

Some product publicity specialists evaluate results by determining the amount of editorial space obtained by publicity on a particular product and comparing that amount of space to other stories or to what competitors have done. This method does not give an indication of whether or not the information was read, much less whether or not it was acted upon. It is more useful as a performance measurement device rather than an evaluation method. As a performance yardstick, it provides one indicator of how well the publicity group is doing its job.

The use of amount of space garnered as an evaluation method is carried one step farther by some. They calculate the cost of the space had it been purchased for advertising. These figures are generally very impressive. But again, they do not indicate whether or not anyone got the message.

Probably the most effective way of evaluating results of product publicity is by analyzing inquiries. Just counting the numbers is not enough, however. An ideal inquiry analysis method might go something like this:

1.   Inquiries are recorded and given a number. The record should include the name of the publication that generated the inquiry.

2.   The inquiry should be qualified by marketing services. That is, a decision has to made whether or not the person who inquired is actually a prospect.

3.   If the inquiry qualifies, it should go to a salesman within a day or two after being received.

4.   The salesman is required to follow up on the inquiry, and after a time to report on whether or not a sale resulted.

Results from such an analysis can be tabulated periodically, possibly once a year, to provide a realistic assessment of results.

Even if the inquiry is not qualified, the individual who made it should receive some kind of reply. This might be sales literature or a polite stock or form letter.

A company should be ready to respond to inquiries before doing publicity on a product. Although this seems to be an obvious point, instances occur in which they are not ready. Prospective customers are irritated when they receive no response, especially if they have a pressing need for the product.

A final point on evaluation of product publicity is that, if it is used, as it should be most of the time, in conjunction with other communications tools, such as advertising, then it should also be evaluated in that conjunction.

Results Reporting

Reporting is a necessary evil in the use of publicity, especially where its usefulness and practice is poorly understood—which is almost everywhere. As James Forrestal once said about his job as secretary of defense, "You not only have to do a good job in this office but people have to believe you're doing a good job."

Clients and executives are interested in results that are reported in terms meaningful to them. Such reports should emphasize the results with a minimum of explanation. Of course, results must be analyzed and interpreted, so some explanation is needed.

It is not necessary to recap an entire publicity project in a report on it, but there may be instances in which it is a good idea to provide an extensive report for educational purposes. When a lengthy report is prepared, results should be summarized at the beginning.

There are many different types of reports. Some that are useful in publicity results reporting are status, project, program, and simple summary reports.

The status report is used to give a play-by-play account of what is being done. Agencies frequently use this type of report to keep clients informed on everything they are doing for them.

The following is a hypothetical status report:

Here is a summary of Kipco publicity work done over the last month:

- Placed a Baltimore tornado photo with *Kitchen Business*. The picture, supplied by the Kipco area sales manager, showed a Kipco cabinet standing amidst the rubble of several homes.
- Case history on telephone "shelfette" units was written and submitted to Bell Telephone Company of Illinois for approval.
- Wrote, secured approvals, and distributed a press release announcing appointment of A. E. Doe as the Milwaukee-Minneapolis area sales manager.
- Arrangements for visit to Philadelphia plant by senior editor of *Home Building Digest*.
- Completed research for a case history story on the use of Kipco standard units in a new line of mobile homes.

Project reports cover individual publicity projects which may single entities or parts of an overall program. The following is a hypothetical report on a publicity project.

Memo to: John Brown, Division Manager

From: Harry Jones, Publicity Director

The publicity project on the lunar power source has been completed. A reprint of the published article is enclosed. The objective, which you set, was to help improve our scientific stature among the space scientists who are concerned with long-term lunar station work. Since our experts were much too busy to write the article, I contracted with a consultant, a scientist, to interview our people and write the article. We put the by-line of our chief scientist on it, and the consultant placed it. When the article was published, we reprinted it and mailed it to key scientists and executives. Our scientists received numerous inquiries about our concept and the work we have done on it. As you know, last week we received a contract from the space agency to continue and accelerate the work. The article opened the door on the project for us.

A program report may be one that covers a multiproject program that has been completed, or one that is a periodic report on an on-going program. The periodic report differs from a status report in that the status report usually covers activity in a more-or-less chronological sequence, while the program report is organized in some formal report format. The following is an example of part of a program report.

1. *Announce Electronegative Gas Detector.* Product releases were mailed to about 80 publications read by potential customers in virtually every major industry in which laboratory equipment is used.
Purpose: To identify potential customers for the product through inquiries.
Results: To date, over 140 qualified inquiries have been processed.
2. *Announce Zero-Impedence Distribution Transformer.* Press conferences held in New York City and Chicago were attended by a total of 18 editors of publications serving the electric utility market.
Purpose: To introduce an important new product to the utility industry; continue to identify the transformer division as a leader in innovation.
Results: To date, 74 inquiries have been received. One of those has resulted in a sale, to Coney Island Electric Company.
3. *Heat Pumps Move North.* Article placed in five publications read by residential builders, heating and air-conditioning contractors, lending organizations, and government agencies concerned with housing.

Purpose: Achieve greater acceptance of the heat pump for heating homes in the North.

Results: The sales department has received inquiries from four major home builders in the North, and 23 air-conditioning and heating contractors.

A simple summary report may be in order if everyone concerned is familiar with the reporting method and with what the summarized results mean in terms of meeting objectives. Such reports are often used to supplement other types of reports. A simple summary report follows.

1972 PUBLICITY RESULTS

Air-Conditioning Division	
Articles published	20
News releases distributed	12
Electronics Division	
Articles published	11
News releases distributed	6
Ordnance Division	
Articles published	2
News releases distributed	2

9

PRIMARY PUBLICITY TOOLS
AND THEIR USE

This chapter, and Chapters 10, 11, and 12, are intended to be read as a unit. They describe the forms of information and tell in some detail how they are produced.

The most common forms of industrial publicity, covered in this chapter, are syndicated information, unsigned exclusive material, and signed exclusive articles. In practice, syndicated information consists mainly of different types of press releases. Examples of most types of information are included.

SYNDICATED INFORMATION

Syndicated material is the most widely used form of industrial publicity information. This and the other forms described here are fairly well defined and proven by practice.

Syndicated material is sent simultaneously to a large number of publications. The press release is the most frequently used syndicated publicity tool. The types of press releases are interpretive, announcement, background information, and photo-and-caption stories.

Interpretive News Release

An interpretive news release reports on some important event or development. It usually depicts a success of some kind and interprets its significance. This type of news release is designed primarily for use in the news columns of business publications.

The interpretive release can be further divided into the event report and the case history. The event report (see Figure 9-1 for example) tells about a significant happening, or a new discovery or technique. The widely used case history (Figure 9-2) release tells about an interesting or useful application of a product or service.

NEWS SERVICE

American Mining Congress

RING BUILDING ● WASHINGTON, D.C. 20036 ● TELEPHONE 202 - 338-2900

J. ALLEN OVERTON, JR., EXECUTIVE VICE PRESIDENT

FOR RELEASE WEDNESDAY A. M., SEPTEMBER 2, 1970

HOYT LAKES, Minn. -- Preparations for the 1970 Christmas Pageant of Peace in the nation's capital are under way here in the iron mining country of northern Minnesota, according to an announcement made by the American Mining Congress in Washington, D. C.

J. Allen Overton, Jr., AMC executive vice president, said 57 balsam fir trees are being selected and tagged by Erie Mining Company to represent the states and territories at the annual Pageant of Peace at the President's Park in Washington. Arrangements for donation of the trees were made by Pickands Mather & Co., Cleveland, Ohio, managing agent for Erie Mining. Pickands Mather is a unit of Diamond Shamrock Corporation, also of Cleveland.

Keith S. Benson, chairman of Pickands Mather, said the trees, which are to be cut in the late fall, illustrate the emphasis the mining industry places on safeguarding environmental values of the nation's mineral areas. Benson said the owners of Erie Mining Company -- Bethlehem Steel Corporation, Youngstown Sheet and Tube Company, The Steel Company of Canada, Limited, and Interlake, Inc. -- have enthusiastically encouraged the

(more)

Figure 9-1. Event report.

118

Corning Glass Works
Public Relations Department
Corning, New York 14830
Tel 607 962-4444

Dennis D. Mog
Sheraton-Park Hotel

1968 Marine Technology Show

Press Information

Application Note: Corning Glass Spheres
                  Provide Flotation For
                  Gulf Stream Measurements

Ten-inch glass spheres fabricated by Corning Glass Works make up the flotation packages for instruments used in a University of Rhode Island study of Gulf Stream currents.

Eighteen spheres are interspaced between sections of a circular buoy resembling a wagon wheel to which a current meter is attached.

Instrument systems using these spheres for flotation have been installed on the ocean floor in the Gulf Stream at depths ranging to 4,000 meters in a region extending from Charleston, S.C., to just beyond Cape Hatteras.

(more)

Figure 9-2. Case history.

Case history information can be used for feature information and for signed articles, which are covered in succeeding sections, and also, in some cases, for advertising. Case history information in the form of a press release runs the risk of little or none of the information being used by the publications to which it is sent. Since the material is syndicated, the publications may feel it does not warrant much space. After all, competing publications will receive the release and may also publish something on the subject.

In some cases, it may be necessary to take the risk and issue case history information as a press release. One reason may be timing. There may be some important reason for having the information printed as quickly as possible, such as an upcoming contract negotiation. Since exclusive case histories usually take longer to appear in print than press release stories, this could be sufficient reason to use the press release form.

If forced by circumstances to issue a press release case history, the graphic aspect should be given special emphasis. Assuming that a press release case history will garner less space, and that important information may be left out, every attempt should be made to provide excellent photos and other illustrations to accompany the release. In cases in which the significant features are not obvious, a skillful photographer or artist may be able to bring out the important aspects.

Announcement Releases

News releases of this type simply tell about some event or product, without much of an attempt to interpret its significance. The types of announcement releases are product and service, business, plant and personnel, and sales literature announcements.

New product announcements include press releases on equipment and services that are, in most cases, entirely new to the customer audience. However, existing types of equipment with significant new features are usually regarded as new products by business publications.

The product announcement is both the most common type of announcement release and the most used form of syndicated information. Figure 9-3 is an example of a release announcing a product; Figure 9-4 an example of a service announcement.

Business publications receive more product announcements than any other type of material from industry, and many of them are misdirected. It is therefore important that product stories be specifically aimed at the categories of publications likely to use them.

Arcair Company
P.O. Box 406
Lancaster, Ohio 43130
Phone: 614-653-5618
S.L. Barnes
Advertising

ARCAIR UNDERWATER CUTTING & WELDING TORCH

Arcair Company, Lancaster, Ohio is introducing a new Underwater Cutting
Torch that may be also used for welding if desired.

This torch, Cat. No. 14-050-101 features a heavy-duty collet enclosed
in a rugged, fluted, insulated locking nut. Insertion or ejection of
an electrode is easily accomplished. This head arrangement which increases
the current contact area, prevents accidental internal arcing since the
electrode is gripped solidly.

There are no physical changes or adjustments necessary to the Torch itself
when changing from a cutting to a welding electrode. It is necessary to
change only the collet to the proper size.

The Torch is equipped with a 5/16" collet to fit metal cutting electrodes.
Additional collets in 5/32" and 3/16" diameter are available for welding
electrodes.

Additional information is available from Arcair Company, P.O. Box 406,
North Memorial Drive, Lancaster, Ohio 43130, S.L. Barnes.

Figure 9-3.   Product announcement.

FOR RELEASE

BE 3-1080

April 13, 1964

RFP's AND SOLE SOURCE NEGOTIATIONS TO BE INCLUDED IN THE DEFENSE MARKET MEASURES SYSTEM (DM^2)

First Step in a Program to Expand DM^2 into a Total Intelligence System

FROST & SULLIVAN, INC. OF NEW YORK, the defense and space industry's source for detailed market statistics, announced today that beginning on April 1, 1964, they will process RFP's (Requests for Proposals) and "Sole Source Negotiations" for RDT&E (research, development, test and evaluation) as an addition to their computerized service, the Defense Market Measures System (DM^2), which during the past three years has provided defense and space market planners with continuous coverage of the contract awards made by the government.   The company announced that this addition to the DM^2 is the first step in a long range program that will provide defense and space market planners with complete market intelligence, fully coded, and on magnetic tape to facilitate retrieval, sorting and calculation with a computer.   The company's goal is, as much as possible, to improve efficiency in the market planning process by replacing the redundant, expensive and cumbersome marketing data storage and retrieval systems now in existence throughout the industry

Pre-award actions, "RFP's" and "Contracts in Negotiation", are considered to be the most urgently needed addition to the present system. Besides being the next earlier phase in the award cycle, they can provide the planner with market intelligence that might not become available again through public sources because of security reasons or because the negotiations were terminated and a contract was never awarded. These pre-award actions can also expand the analysts knowledge of competition, the state of the art, and of the location and nature of the customers in a given market segment.

Figure 9-4.   Service announcement.

122

A side benefit of product releases is that they can sometimes be used for a type of product marketing research. Inquiries resulting from a product release can be classified and used to determine the interest in and reception of the product in its potential market. Sales may even result if the people who inquire are contacted and their specific requirements met.

It is essential that some type of information be available to respond to inquiries resulting from publication of press releases. A company can hurt its reputation by disappointing customers who request additional information.

The second type of announcement release, the business announcement, is usually about orders, business milestones, new contracts, or financial affairs such as earnings. Such releases are usually designed to go to business publications that cover the financial and management aspects of industry. An example of a business announcement is shown in Figure 9-5.

Announcements of financial conditions, sales, profits, and so on, can help influence the price of stocks (up *or* down). They can be used to prepare the financial community for stock issues, and to improve a company's stature with investors, bankers, and brokers. They can also lead to trouble if they are not written and handled within the framework of Security Exchange Commission regulations.

Plant and personnel announcements describe such events as new plant openings, plant expansions, personnel appointments, and organizational changes.

Sales literature announcements (Figure 9-6 is an example) are cut-and-dried news releases designed only to obtain mention in the "literature available" sections of business publications and thereby stimulate requests for the literature.

Photo-and-Caption Releases

Short news releases consisting of photos and captions are a common publicity tool. One way they are used is to enable publications to cover something relatively unnewsworthy but photographically interesting. Another way they can be used is to put out information on something that cannot be covered in depth because of proprietary aspects, sensitivity, security classification, or other restrictions. Figure 9-7 is an example of a photo-and-caption release.

Because this type of release is based on a photo, it is essential to obtain the best possible pictures. This means using a photographer who knows industrial publicity photography. In addition, mass-producing prints of the

W.'L. VERGASON/OFFICE OF PUBLIC INFORMATION/MELBOURNE, FLA. 32902/PHONE (OFFICE) 305/723-1511 (HOME) 305/727-3819

RADIATION-WESTINGHOUSE SIGN
SALES, SERVICE AGREEMENT

MELBOURNE, Fla. --- Radiation Service Company, a subsidiary of Radiation Incorporated, has entered into an agreement with
Westinghouse Electric Corporation to sell, lease, install and maintain
electronic teaching aids manufactured by the firm.

The announcement by Radiation follows a Westinghouse statement
made earlier this month that it is entering the educational electronics
market. Westinghouse said it is developing a line of electronic audio-
visual equipment for schools, colleges, and industrial firms.

Radiation Service Company will market Westinghouse equipment
in Florida, Maryland, Delaware, New Jersey, Pennsylvania, Ohio,
Indiana, Illinois, and the District of Columbia.

* * *

FOR RELEASE: January 26, 1967   NEWS

Figure 9-5. Business announcement.

Westinghouse **Catalog News**

R. J. Benke 314-210N
Phone: (412) 255-3321

June 3, 1970

For Immediate Use

BROCHURES DESCRIBE MINICOMPUTER HARDWARE

The P-2000 process input/output system, P-2000 card punch,
and P-2000 line printer for the Prodac® 2000 Series Computing Control
Systems are described in three illustrated publications. The Prodac
2000 is the Westinghouse minicomputer announced early last year.

DB-23-204, a twelve-page bulletin on the P-2000 process input/
output system, gives a detailed description of the operation of the
system and lists its features. Included is a description on the five
main avenues of communication between the P-2000 computer and the process
being controlled: contact inputs, contact outputs, interrupts, analog
inputs and analog outputs.

DB-23-701 is a four-page publication on the P-2000 card punch.
Topics included are advantages of the new system, operational procedure,
and specifications.

The four-page DB-23-702 describes how the P-2000 line printer
operates and lists the advantages and specifications of the equipment.
It also gives a step-by-step procedure for operating the machine.

For copies of DB-23-204, DB-23-701 and DB-23-702 from the
Hagan/Computer Systems Division, write Westinghouse Electric Corporation,
P.O. Box 868, Pittsburgh, Pa. 15230.

###

COPIES OF DB-23-204, DB-23-701 AND DB-23-702 ENCLOSED.

Technical Publicity
Westinghouse Electric Corporation
Box 2278 Pittsburgh Pa. 15230
Area Code 412   491-2800

Figure 9-6.   Literature announcement.

Figure 9-7. Photo release.

photos for distribution must be done by a photo lab that is able to maintain something approaching the quality of the original pictures.

Some publications, such as newsletters, do not use photos, and in certain cases do not even want to receive them. This desire should of course be honored.

Fact Sheets

The fact sheet can be used to give detailed information on equipment or facilities. For example, in a product announcement or a plant opening announcement release, excessive detail can make the story boring and hard to read. The fact sheet lends itself well to such a situation. Enclosed with a release, it provides details beyond those in the release for anyone who is interested.

Another situation in which the fact sheet is useful is during on-going events when conditions are changing rapidly. Examples of such events are major construction projects, space flights, and mine disasters. Fact sheets for such events can either made up in advance and updated periodically, or put together quickly during the event. In an emergency situation, they can be used in lieu of a press release or official statement. There may even be occasions when it is advantageous to stick to fact sheets alone.

Background Information

Background information (Figure 9-8) is detailed, lengthy material usually sent to many publications simultaneously. One of its purposes is to let publications know the company has a particular capability or product line, and thereby stimulate editor inquiries. Another purpose is to provide material for the background files of the publications in anticipation of future coverage. Yet another purpose is to explain exotic or unfamiliar areas or techniques to help magazine editors report accurately and give proper credit. This is occasionally necessary when a company is involved in a field so new or so specialized that even well-informed editors do not understand the accomplishments.

Background information is usually specially prepared for distribution to the press. In some cases, it may be appropriate to use other types of information, such as a technical paper or an article prepared for a company publication.

UNSIGNED EXCLUSIVE MATERIAL

Written material submitted for the use of a single publication but without an author's by-line is unsigned exclusive material. It is long enough to go into considerable detail, and is usually more specialized than most press releases. This type of material is an excellent tool which is underutilized by most companies.

Feature Information

One form of unsigned exclusive information is feature information. Supplied to a single publication, it usually is used for an article developed by a member of the staff of the publication. Sometimes an article based on such information appears under the by-line of a member of the magazine staff.

Feature information fulfills the need of most publications for more

ALSEP Press Backgrounder

**Apollo
Lunar
Surface
Experiments
Package**

Bendix Aerospace
Systems Division

Figure 9-8. Background information.

material than they have the resources to obtain through their own efforts. In some cases, it should be specially prepared for particular publications. Its reception will be far better than that of stock material.

One type of feature information is state-of-the-art or survey report material which describes a technique, a product, or a service. It is usually prepared and supplied especially to obtain coverage in known "round-up" or forecast articles.

Case history articles are probably the most common form of feature information. They describe the *use* of a technique, a product, or a service. Companies involved in high-volume manufacture and not selling directly to consumers usually have ready-made media to talk about their products in the form of one or more vertical or specialized publications that serve them. They frequently also have one or more horizontal publications also serving the market. Such publications use case history information showing their readers how others solve their problems.

The exclusive case history is related to the press release case history. As indicated in the section on press releases, it is often best to use the exclusive in order to obtain adequate coverage in one key publication. There are, however, several other alternatives. One is to use both a press release and an exclusive. In this case, the exclusive is placed for publication, and a shorter version issued as a press release at or after the time the exclusive is published.

Another wrinkle is to simultaneously offer a semiexclusive to the leading publications in several different fields. With this method, it is necessary to tell the editors contacted how the story is being handled. Also, the names of the other publications contacted should be given.

In using the semiexclusive method, it is very useful to know the publications well enough to be able to predict how the editors will react. Some are used to this approach and do not resent it. Others are slightly offended but go along with it. A few dislike the technique enough to not go along with it.

Photo Features

Related to the straight feature is the exclusive photo feature which fulfills the need of publications for good photos to add interest to their pages. These features consist of one or more photos with just enough supporting information to tell what the photos are and the significance of what is pictured. Mainly for use in the news columns of publications, the photos are submitted in the form of black and white prints unless a publication specifically requests color.

One situation in which the photo feature is a particularly valuable tool is in the case in which there is but one primary publication that covers the field of interest.

Special photos for use on the covers of magazines can be considered a type of photo feature. Cover photos of a company's products or people can be extremely valuable. Every reader looks at the cover, and different issues of a magazine are often identified by what appears on it. The "readership" of a cover is higher by a considerable factor than any other part of the magazine.

Photos for cover use are usually in the form of color transparencies. Many publications are beginning to accept sharp 35-millimeter transparencies, but some still insist on larger sizes. Most editors will not consider color prints because of the loss of resolution between the color print and the final printed page.

Given the objective of placing a color photo for use on the cover of a magazine, the best method is as follows. A photographer who is a specialist in industrial publicity should be assigned to the job. He should be given examples of covers appearing on several past issues of the magazine. Photos should be taken that express both the photographer's and the publicity expert's viewpoint of what shots are important. A view, or preferably three or four views, should be selected jointly by the publicity specialist and the photographer. Color prints and transparencies should then be produced. The print is to help the magazine editor and art director to visualize how the photo will look in printed form, and the transparency is for use in printing.

More often than not, cover photos are tied in with feature articles in the magazine. The publicity man can do several things to take advantage of this fact. First, if he finds out what the magazine, or magazines, of immediate interest to his company or client are going to be featuring, he can be prepared with special photos to offer to the magazine. Second, he can try whenever he places a story with the magazine to supply color photos especially intended for cover use.

SIGNED EXCLUSIVE ARTICLES

Many business publications depend upon outside contributors for the long, detailed articles they use. This demand is an opportunity for companies to satisfy a need of the publications and at the same time demonstrate some capability or show the advantages of a product.

Signed exclusive articles are specialized, long, and detailed articles written usually by, but sometimes for, scientists, engineers, or other professionals to help their organization, for professional recognition, or both. Articles written primarily for professional recognition are referred to here as signed professional articles. Those written primarily to put out a message a company wants its audiences to hear are called business support articles. The distinction between the two is that the business support article is deliberately planned and executed, while the professional article, although perhaps encouraged by, does not originate from marketing or business strategy.

Professional Signed Articles

Professional signed articles are necessary, and companies should encourage their production. Professionals need articles as one outlet to achieve professional recognition and to help them in their own professional development. In addition to the professional recognition and development aspect, articles of this type help build or maintain a company's identity in its field.

One very important result of a signed article, its affect on morale, is often overlooked. If it is part of a progressive professional development policy, a signed article program can help convince professionals that the company is a good place to work. This encourages them to stay with the company. Another result is that it may be helpful in recruiting.

Many companies with a high technology content in their business have official signed-article programs. The stated purpose of one such program is to improve the firm's reputation in the scientific and technical community. The engineers and scientists in that community will, the reasoning goes, influence their management which may include the company's customers.

Some companies consider the identity-building aspect so important that they offer an incentive in the form of an assured honorarium. Some publications pay for articles, but many do not. In fact, some association and society journals levy page charges against their authors to help support the publication.

Companies that provide an honorarium incentive are those that have a need to communicate in detail and in depth their capabilities in their field. One risk in a reward system is that some articles produced purely for the reward are poorly written and have contents of questionable value. Such articles may be difficult to place, and even if eventually published may contribute little or nothing toward improving the company's identity.

The following example explains one company's signed article program.

Articles for Industrial, Technical, and Business Magazines
These magazines use articles that aim to inform, instruct, persuade, or a combination of these. There are three main types of articles.

1. Application articles which are most often about methods or equipment. The "how-to" article is in this category.
2. Development articles which report new information and interpret its significance.
3. State-of-the-art or survey articles which keep the lines of communication open between members of an industry or an area of specialization.

Authors of articles for industrial, technical, and business magazines should strive to write for the readers of the magazines at which they are aiming. The readers are looking for mainly one kind of material: information that will help them to do their jobs better.

Benefits to Authors

- Published articles enhance professional standing. Prestige and recognition gained from publication of an article in a leading magazines are a lasting and significant reward.
- Writing articles trains an individual in orderly thinking, improves writing ability, and adds to the person's storehouse of knowledge.
- Published articles contribute to advancement of the author's profession. By writing articles, he shares his specialized knowledge with his fellow professionals and adds to the body of specialized knowledge.
- Authors receive modest cash honorariums for published articles they write. If the magazine does not pay, and a few do not, the company does. Checks usually range from $35 to $100.

Benefits to the Company

- Quality articles by employees that appear in key magazines improve the stature of the company. They create a preference for the company in the minds of customers and help build a better image. The stature and reputation of the company helps sell products and services.

Approvals

After a manuscript is completed, it is turned over to the publicity director who obtains company and customer approvals and then submits the article for publication.

Business Support Article

The business support article is an excellent industrial publicity tool which is not used to the extent that it might be. It should be part of most industrial publicity programs. It is an opportunity to provide a type of information that specialized publications need, and at the same time have the company mentioned and associated with the subject matter. There is always a demand for good articles, since many business magazines have difficulty finding enough good articles to publish.

One of the advantages of the business support article is that just by being published the article is in a sense sanctioned by an editor who is an expert in the field and is presumed to be objective. The article therefore gains a degree more creditability than advertising, sales literature, and sales pitches. Another advantage is that the entire story can be told in enough detail to prove the point even if the subject is highly technical.

This type of article is often written by assignment when the boss tells the author to produce it. Sometimes, such articles are ghostwritten.

After publication, this type of article is often reprinted and distributed as a handout or as a direct mail piece, and sometimes is used as an appendix for a sales proposal. The cost of reprinting is negligible in comparison with that of preparing and printing a new piece of sales literature which might be designed to do the same job as an article reprint. Nearly all publications have a reprinting service. Reprint costs start at about 1/2¢ per copy and go up from there, varying with length, quality, and quantity. In some cases, it costs less if reprints are ordered before the issue of the magazine is printed.

Some companies have preprinted covers (Figure 9-9 is an example) for reprints that carry the company's logotype. They reprint the articles themselves or have a local printer do it. In this case, they should obtain permission from the publication because of the copyright law. A minority of publications will not grant this permission; they prefer to do all reprinting themselves for two reasons. First, there is in most cases a slight profit to the magazine. Second, some editors are concerned about how companies handle reprints. They do not want their editorial material to be reprinted in a format that makes it look like a testimonial by the publication for a product or company. When permission is granted, the publications nearly always ask that the reprint carry their credit line. A typical credit line is the one required by McGraw-Hill: "Reprinted from *Electronics,* October 16, 1967; Copyright © 1967, McGraw-Hill, Inc.; All Rights Reserved."

Signed Articles, Special Advantage Of

There are some situations in which the signed article is the best way of putting a certain message across. For example, it may be the best way of reaching a special segment of the scientific community. Many scientists have an aversion to anything that seems commercially inspired. Informing

Side-Look Radar Provides a New Tool for Topographic and Geological Surveys

Reprinted from Nov. 1972 Issue of
Westinghouse ENGINEER

Westinghouse Aerospace and
Electronic Systems

P. O. Box 746
Baltimore, Maryland 21203
(301) 765-4485

Reprint 115

Produced by
Westinghouse Technical Information

Figure 9-9. Reprint.

by implication through a scholarly article may be what is needed to reach such scientists.

One company wanted to build an identity as a contender for space-related business beyond the time of the manned space-flight programs. It had some in-house and some government-funded research and development work aimed at that time period. It decided that a series of articles on these research programs was the approach to use. It turned out in discussions with the scientists that they felt they were too busy to take the time to write such articles. There was also an element of disinterest involved. An outside consultant writer was found who had a doctorate and was himself a scientist. The initial article was on a lunar phenomenom that indicated a possible power source. The writer made three visits to the company to obtain the information he needed. He first drafted a lengthy expository outline which was used by the company's publicity man in finding a publication that was interested. The second publication queried was interested. The writer completed the article, and it was published. His fee, including expenses, was $400, but that was several years ago. At present rates, the cost would be at least double that. The company reprinted the article for about $75 and mailed it to key government and scientific people. The article was considered by the company's management to be a success and well worth the expenditure.

In another situation, a business-minded engineering executive who had a doctorate and was a world-renowned specialist in the design of electronic filters wrote an article on the design of a particular type of filter network. The company's publicity man arranged to have the article published in a major electronic magazine. Several months later, the executive's company was awarded a contract for a multimillion-dollar communications system. The executive felt that his article was the deciding factor in the company's winning the contract. The article had proved that the company could do what it had said it could do in its proposal. The customer had previously been convinced that the proposed method was not feasible. In the article, however, the executive had the space to develop the concept and to present important data that had been impossible to put before the customer before. In addition, the article had a high degree of credibility, since it had the blessing of the editors of a highly respected publication in the field who were electronic engineering experts in their own right.

Signed Article Procedure

Things that must be taken into account when the idea of a signed article is considered are the objective, the audience, available resources, and the publication potential of the article. The idea of starting with an objective cannot be emphasized enough. One publicity expert says:

Once is a while someone comes by and says something like "Wouldn't it be a good idea to have an article on such and such published." When you ask them,

"Why?" more often than not you get a blank stare followed by a belligerent answer like "Because it would be good for us!" and you can see they are itching to add to the end of the sentence the noun "stupid." Time after time, they get the cart before the horse.

Once the objective and audience are defined, it must be determined if the manpower (or the money to pay for assistance) is available, and it must be established that there actually is a market for the proposed article. The latter means that someone has to determine what publications serve the target audience and what kind of material these publications use.

After the preliminary questions have been answered, an article proposal is prepared. This might consist of an outline in topical or in expository form, or it might be in the form of existing information such as a paper, a report, or a technical memorandum. The type of information most magazines need for their evaluation is indicated in Figure 9-10, an article proposal form that *Electronic Design* magazine asks potential authors to use. This form asks the author to summarize the article, and to list his qualifications, the reason he feels the magazine's readers would be interested, illustrations to be used, projected length, and projected completion date.

The article is usually submitted to the top editor of a magazine, whether his title is editor-in-chief, executive editor, or just editor. In the case of a magazine with a large staff, and when it is known which department editor will eventually evaluate the article proposal, it often saves time to submit it directly to the department editor.

Making a personal visit to an editor to submit an article proposal or preceding the submittal by a telephone call is usually a waste of time. If, however, the project is extremely important, it could be beneficial to hand carry the proposal to be sure there is no misunderstanding about it, and to offer full cooperation in getting the article written, illustrated, and into the editor's hands.

The submittal letter should not attempt to convince the editor to use the article. It may be necessary to explain the subject if the editor is not completely familiar with it, or if the proposal material is not completely adequate.

The submittal letter needs only to say that the material is being submitted for evaluation as the subject of an exclusive article for the magazine. The working title and the name of the author should also be mentioned.

The editor rejects the idea, gives an unqualified expression of interest, or says he is interested if certain requirements are met. In the vast majority of

Electronic Design   ARTICLE PROPOSAL FORM

HAYDEN PUBLISHING COMPANY, INC.   850 THIRD AVE., NEW YORK, N.Y. 10022   PL 1-5530

   Before writing your article for ELECTRONIC DESIGN, fill out and send us
this form, giving as much detailed data as possible. An editor will review
your proposal promptly and suggest any desired revisions. You can then use
the accepted proposal as your guide in writing the final article.

1. ARTICLE TITLE (Make it descriptive enough to tell what your article is
   about):_____

   _____

2. ARTICLE CONTENT (A detailed outline with enough information to permit
   proper evaluation of your proposed article):_____

   _____

   _____

   _____

   _____

   _____

   _____

   _____

   _____

   _____

   _____

   _____

   _____

3. READER INTEREST (Why should readers be interested in your article?)

   _____

   _____

4. ILLUSTRATIONS (How many diagrams, photos, etc.?)_____

5. ARTICLE LENGTH (Note: A standard 8-1/2" x 11," double-spaced, typewrit-
   ten page contains about 250 words):_____

6. AUTHOR DATA: Name_____Title_____
   Company_____
   Address_____Zip Code_____

cases, editors will not commit themselves actually to publishing an article until they have the final manuscript and find it acceptable.

Once a publication is interested, the author can proceed with the writing of the article. Magazines often supply writing guides which are useful to authors. In addition, the author should go through some back issues of the magazine and read articles that are similar to the one he is writing. Some additional hints on writing and illustrating articles are given in Chapters 11 and 13.

After the final manuscript is submitted to the magazine, it is edited for publication. It is then returned to an author or his representative for review to be sure that incorrect information or a wrong slant was not introduced in editing.

Forms of the Signed Article

There are various forms of the signed article, whether business support or professional. One useful form much in demand and one of the most common in print is the how-to or application article. This tells the reader, directly or indirectly, how to do something in his work better, faster, or for less cost. This fits in with the basic purpose of most business publications, the presentation of information of direct use to the readers.

The how-to article describes a technique or product, and in the process shows the reader how to apply it. This approach must be kept in mind when the article is being written. This is not as easy as it sounds. In the vast majority of cases, authors who are not writers (i.e., their work is something other than writing, such as engineering), find it very hard to shift from what seems to be their natural mental framework to the viewpoint of the reader. Too often, these authors tend to want to write "how we did it" rather than "here's how to do it."

The case history is another well-known type of signed article. In organization and purpose, it resembles the press release and feature information case history material covered in previous sections. In certain cases, evaluation of the information, the media, and the audience may indicate that a signed article is the best means of accomplishing the objective.

Case history signed articles that carry the signature of a satisfied customer (even though the article may have been written for him) can be an effective method of demonstrating to other customers a company's ability to solve their problems.

Advantages of this approach are believability of a customer-authored article "sanctioned" by an editor, drawing upon the best source of information available on application of the product or service to a particular type of problem, acceptance on the part of a publication since it provides a basic type of material which helps readers do their jobs better. Another advantage is that it helps maintain or improve relations with the original customer.

The following is one procedure for getting a customer-signed case history article written.

First, an application is found that shows to best advantage the company's capability or the features of a product. The salesman on the job is consulted on the question of who in the customer organization is the appropriate person to approach. The potential author is contacted and an article proposed. Assurances are given that the author will receive whatever degree of assistance he needs, from photography and artwork right up through ghostwriting of the entire article. The potential author is also assured that he will have full review, approval, and veto rights.

If the potential author agrees to the plan, he should be asked to find out if his bosses also agree.

The next step is to select and query a publication in the field that is interested in the type of product or service to be covered in the article. Here again, it is important to note the importance of the audience. The magazine has to be selected on the basis of the number of potential customers in the readership.

An outline in either expository or topical form can be used for the query. It is important to be sure that the publication queried will mention the name of the company in the final article. Some publications have a policy against this. They are few in number, but it is important to know.

One company went to a lot of trouble and spent not a little money to produce a case history on a certain type of equipment for a broadcasting station. They obtained information from the station's engineering manager, photographed the installation, and wrote the article putting the engineering manager's name on it. The article was submitted to the publication selected as being the one with the greatest readership among the audience to be reached and was quickly accepted. When published, the article appeared virtually unchanged, indicating that the company had done a good job of anticipating the magazine's requirements. The only significant change the editor had made was to eliminate the company's name from the body of the article. With one small pencil stroke, the editor had rendered the article practically worthless for the company. It is important to note, however, that it was the company's mistake, not the editor's.

Once a publication is interested, another conference with the potential author is in order. Final agreements are made on how information will be gathered, the article will be written, photos will be taken, and approvals will be obtained.

Several back issues of the publication should be reviewed before writing begins, and articles similar to the one contemplated should be read thoroughly and analyzed. The article should be written so that the company's message is strongly implied but not explicitly stated. Many of the techniques of article writing covered in a later section on the preparation of signed exclusive articles also apply to this type of article.

10
OTHER PUBLICITY TOOLS
AND THEIR USE

In addition to the common forms of publicity covered in the previous chapter, there are other kinds of information, or informational activities, that represent publicity opportunities. Often overlooked, they are sometimes more practical and more effective as publicity tools than the more common forms. Publicity planning is incomplete without at least a consideration of these other forms.

INFORMATION FOR ELECTRONIC MEDIA

In some cases, television is considered essential to a company's communications program. There are some things in the way of publicity that can be done. One is to send press releases to the news directors of stations. If the story has a strong news angle, it may be worthwhile contacting the news directors personally.

Another thing that can be done is to maintain contact with key network directors, producers, editors, and correspondents. To do this effectively, it is almost a necessity to use the services of a New York public relations representative or a public relations agency.

Yet another approach is to supply television film clips and radio reports to major television and radio stations. These are short news reports, typically a minute or so in length.

Television film clips can be produced in black and white or in color, with or without sound. A script should be supplied with the film clip even if it has sound. This gives the station the option of using the sound on the film or having a newscaster read the script.

Television clips can be placed exclusively or can be syndicated widely to as many as 200 or 300 stations. Reply cards can accompany syndicated clips with a request that the stations return them indicating whether or not the clip was used.

Some companies have used television film clips for many years as a publicity tool. They have had mixed success. One tendency seems to be that major city stations report using clips with less frequency than stations in smaller cities.

Radio reports can take one of two forms. Information can be taped on cassettes and supplied to stations in a manner similar to the way television film clips are handled. The second way is a live report. Such a report can be called in from a location where something is happening. The publicity man simply calls the news director or news desk of a station, tells him what is happening, and asks if he would like to have a report, called a voice feed, from the site. A hypothetical case might be the testing in Nevada of a new type of rocket engine manufactured in Anytown, New Jersey. The publicity man could call the Anytown stations from Nevada with a short voice feed. He would have to have an actuality, which might be the roar of the engine being tested, the program manager saying a few words about the test. Stations usually have a seperate number for voice feeds. The publicity man would call that number after getting a go-ahead from the news director and would read a prepared statement accompanied by an appropriate actuality.

SPEECHES

Publicity associated with speeches is a form not widely used, but is particularly useful for some kinds of firms. One example is the type of company that supplies equipment or services to municipalities. Since there are numerous opportunities for speeches on the local level, such a company has a ready-made forum for its messages, as demonstrated by the following example.

> An engineering company has as one of its areas of business municipal water system planning and design. The chief engineer of the company is an excellent speaker, and makes himself available to civic organizations and other groups to talk about water resources, pollution, water supply systems, and so on.

Publicizing Speeches

Making a speech is actually a way of creating news. In some cases, it is possible to capitalize extensively upon a speech to obtain a significant amount of publicity. This can enlarge the audience of the speech from dozens to thousands. If this is the desired effect, a publicity project must be planned in connection with the speech.

The publicity project for a speech begins before the speech is written. The desired publicity result of the speech is formulated and used as one of the criteria for writing the speech.

Once the speech is prepared and the arrangements for giving it are finalized, the publicity man should contact the organization sponsoring the speech to see if they intend to publicize it, and to offer to help in any way possible. Such offers of help are usually accepted. The publicity man should always work through the host organization, even when he does all the work.

Lists of all newspapers, wire service offices, interested local or regional magazines, appropriate business publications, and television and radio stations are prepared. A letter is sent by the sponsoring organization, preferably on its letterhead, and signed by a member of the organization. The letter gives a brief summary of the subject of the talk, the name of the speaker, and the time and place it will be given. The final paragraph should invite the editor, reporter, or correspondent to attend. It should give the name and telephone number of someone to contact for further information. This letter should go out 2 or 3 weeks in advance of the date of the speech. A reply card may be enclosed asking the invitees whether or not they plan to attend and requesting that they return the card. Those that do not respond should be called about a week before the speech date.

The same information as is given in the letter is put into a press release issued a week or so before the event. If any weekly newspapers are among the invited press group, the mailing date should be early enough to give the weeklies a chance to run an announcement of the speech. A biographical sketch of the speaker's background and a photo of him should accompany the release.

A more detailed news release is prepared far enough ahead of the engagement date so that it can be put into the hands of the invited press group a day or two in advance of the speech.

Press Relations

If enough of the press group plan to attend, a section of seats or a table should be set up for them at a good location in the room. Copies of the speech and press release should be available to the press representatives.

A question-and-answer session is nearly always a good idea. Most speakers are reasonably good at responding to questions. If the speaker is not, then the question-and-answer session becomes less advantageous.

Additional Use of a Speech

After the speech, the subject is not usually dead. If the information is of any real significance beyond being a good speech topic, it may become the basis of a signed article.

> A value analysis engineer gave a talk before a meeting of a small group of city officials. The subject was a value analysis project for a large city. It was the first time the highly specialized industrial technique of value analysis had been used for such a municipal study. The engineer's remarks were used by his publicity man to see if any of the municipal magazines would be interested. One was interested, and an article eventually was published.

Adaptable Speeches

Speeches are a necessary part of the communications effort of some companies. In these cases, it is often a good idea to prepare a master script with future needs in mind. It should be made up of units that can be included or left out, interchanged, or substituted as needs dictate. To make speeches more interesting and understandable, a library of appropriate visuals should be built up so that selections can be made to illustrate the basic speech and its modifications.

Many companies do not have anyone with speech writing experience. In cases in which the need for good speeches is critical and in-house speech writing expertise is nonexistent, the company should call upon a professional. Even when the need for speeches is not critical, a speech writer can provide invaluable help by preparing a basic speech.

Visuals

The place where many speeches fall short is in the area of visuals. Some of the mechanical shortcomings are numbers and words too small to be easily read by the audience, too much material cramped into too little space, illegible information, dull illustrations, and an uninteresting format.

Once a speaker is conscious of such shortcomings, he can correct them himself or may feel it is necessary to call in a consultant to liven up the presentation.

Equipment presently available permits the use of three screens (or one large screen for three images) and any combination of two slide projectors and a movie projector. Such a presentation provides a fast-moving, highly interesting visual accompaniment for a talk.

Still on the subject of equipment, it should be noted that the popular opaque projector has limitations. Situations in which it is most useful are informal or extemporaneous talks and talks before small groups. The speaker may be responding to frequent questions and may have cause to refer back to illustrations previously used. Also, he may have some reason to make notes on the illustrations as he goes along. Rolls of transparent plastic sheeting are available for these projectors. Using a grease pencil for writing or drawing on the plastic sheeting allows the projector to be used in lieu of a blackboard.

PAPERS

Technical and specialized papers are usually written for presentation before meetings, conferences, and symposia sponsored by societies, associations, and other special-interest organizations. They are sometimes written especially for publication in the official journal of an organization. Papers written for presentation are frequently published as proceedings or transactions.

Usually, reports or highly specialized work papers appeal to very narrow audiences of experts in particular fields. Such papers can be, but seldom are, used as a communications tool for telling a specialist audience about a highly technical or otherwise esoteric capability a company may possess. Sometimes papers are the only way to communicate such a message. Some technologies are so unfamiliar and complicated that only a small number of specialists can understand them. The following example illustrates another instance in which the paper is useful as a communications tool.

A company developed a remarkably good camera for military and space use. Because it was small and precise and had new features no other cameras had, the device was very expensive, far beyond the reach of even the most ardent hobbyists and most conscientious professionals. Therefore the company had no intention of selling the camera on the open market. They were looking to apply their know-how to develop custom-built cameras for special applications.

The company knew from past experience that if they used standard communications techniques the camera would be given the wrong kind of coverage and they would be deluged by inquiries from not only serious hobbyists and professionals but everyone from school kids to little old ladies and even prisoners. Even if they had wanted to respond to the inquiries, they would not have had the resources.

There was an audience of customers they did want to reach, however, and they used the technical paper as the main means of reaching them. They presented a paper on the camera at a conference where the type of people they wanted to reach would be present. They also bought exhibit space at the conference and demonstrated the camera. A press release was issued to a selective list of business publications. It said that the camera was being described in a paper at the conference. That statement was key to the release. It assured that the story would probably not appear in the product section of any magazines. If anywhere, it would appear in the news columns. The release throughout emphasized the high performance, special-application nature of the camera, and stated that the camera was developed only for military and aerospace programs.

Another thing this example shows is that a presented paper is another type of news opportunity. If the paper is on a subject related to a publicity objective, and if there is anything at all newsworthy about it, a press release should be prepared.

A press release (Figure 10-1) on the paper will announce the news to publications that are not represented at the meeting, or whose representatives missed the session at which the paper was presented. It also serves to interpret the significance of the paper in case the editors and writers missed it.

Another reason for using the paper as a communications tool is the motivation of engineers and scientists. They tend to hold a paper in higher regard than they do an article for a business publication. In their eyes it has a more professional tone than the article. And, in the final analysis, engineers and scientists very often have an ambivalence about working in industry. Many, if not most, identify more with their profession than with their company. So it is not surprising to find that they are frequently more receptive to the idea of a paper than to the idea of an article for a business publication.

One company made a study of their paper and article output for a year. They found that their engineers and scientists wrote one paper for every 12 individuals and one article for every 21 individuals. They produced only 45 percent as many articles as papers. Interestingly, the company had an assured honorarium policy for articles but not for papers.

A Limitation of Papers

It is important to note that, when a paper is presented (even though it may not even be written but given from notes), it is considered to have been published from both the legal and ethical viewpoints. This of course influences whatever additional use is made of a paper. For example, it

TRW SYSTEMS

TRW INC. · *ONE SPACE PARK* · *REDONDO BEACH, CALIFORNIA 90278* · *AREA CODE 213-679-8711*

CONTACT: C. H. Wacker, Ext. 11771   FOR RELEASE: May 18, 1966

Technical Paper Summary
National Aerospace Electronics Conference

USE OF INTERPRETIVE COMPUTER SIMULATIONS
By
Howard Grossman
Member of the Technical Staff
Electronic Systems Division

TRW Systems
(An Operating Group of TRW Inc.)
Redondo Beach, California

DAYTON, Ohio, May 18, 1966 -- Will the bird fly home? This critical question about interplanetary missions depends for its answer on the accuracy of the computer program in each space vehicle. To aid in the verification of these programs, Interpretive Computer Simulations (ICS) are designed and effectively used. The ICS recreates the computers real time performance during flight. It has diagnostic capabilities far greater than the real computer. These capabilities allow ICS to detect errors that might go unnoticed.

Reduction of schedule time and contract costs, and better checkout confidence were achieved by using the all digital ICS method at TRW Systems for the program checkout of: Atlas, Minuteman, Titan, Ranger, Mariner, Mercury, Centaur, and LEM/AGS. ICS's can aid in the verification of guidance programs, communication and computer test programs, integration and calibration routines, and it can help perform post-flight evaluation of the computer's performance during the mission.

- more -

Figure 10-1. Release on a paper.

147

usually cannot be submitted to a magazine for full publication in its presented form. However, one way it can be used is as the basis of an article, and if substantially rewritten can then be published. Another way is to offer the paper to business publications for abstracting so that they can report upon it in their news columns.

SHOWS AND MEETINGS

Trade shows, conferences, and conventions that have exhibits are considered by many to offer considerable publicity potential. The proponents of this point of view say that editors of publications in the field faithfully attend the shows and are more accessible than at any other time. Also, they say, companies very often push development of a product or refinement of a capability to try to have it ready for a particular show where large numbers of their customers are gathered together and will see and stop to discuss the product. Since this event is the first showing of such products, the reasoning goes, it should also be the place where they are announced to the press. Therefore publicity, and maybe even a press conference, is in order.

Publicity-at-Show Limitations

The arguments for publicity during a show are true to varying degrees for different types of shows. However, there are some significant factors that often mitigate against the effectiveness of the trade show as the best place to initiate publicity. Among them are the sheer number of products being shown, many for the first time, and the intense competition for the time of the editors who are in attendance. Editors go to shows to hear the papers or speeches being presented, to report on them, and to see what is new in the exhibits. Also, companies compete for their time with invitations to press conferences, hospitality rooms, and interviews of company marketing managers, engineering managers, product managers, general managers, and even presidents. What it boils down to is the company who gets there first with the most is the one that obtains the coverage.

As a general rule, therefore, if a company is not ready far in advance and preplaces material and sends out invitations far in advance, it is probably wasting its time and money in trying to obtain editorial attention at a show.

As do all general rules, this one has its exceptions. The main one is that if a company has a truly exceptional product or an otherwise outstanding story to tell, and if it is brought to the attention of the editors, it will obtain coverage. However, such exceptional cases are quite rare, on the order of 1 in 1000.

Another exception is when the show or meeting is a small, specialized event. At very large shows—such as some petroleum, electronic, and residential building conferences—there is a wide spread of interests and products represented. Also, there is a wide spectrum of business publications represented. The chance of a company going unrecognized in such an environment is greater than at the smaller shows where all the participants, exhibitors, and press representatives have a common interest in a more specialized area. The Hydro-Products press release shown in Figure 10-2 is a good example of information released at such a show, the Marine Technology Society Conference.

Preshow Publicity

Lacking an earth-shaking story, the best alternative is to be early. Ideally, if a new product or service is to be announced for the first time at an exhibit, publicity should be initiated about 60 days in advance of the show. In this way, the story will receive more attention from the editors than the competing stories put out at the time of the show when there is a glut on the market. If the story is not disseminated, or if placement is not attempted until the time of the show, it is likely to be lost in the crowd.

Another argument for being early is that, even when stories are published in a show issue, they are probably not as effective as in other issues because the readership of the show issues is lower than normal. This is due to many of the readers being involved in the show and so busier than usual, and because the show issues are larger than normal, making it more difficult for their readers to go through them.

Many publications have an issue that gives advance coverage of a show. These appear as much in advance as a month, depending on how well the show and the magazine's publication schedule coincide. This is the issue to place the story in. As indicated, this means putting the story out about 60 days in advance of the show, the exact time depending on the closing dates of the interested publications and the date of the show.

Publicity Activity during a Show

Despite the drawbacks to publicity work during a show, there may be good reasons for going about it in just that way. One reason might be that the marketing manager wants it that way. Another, very common, reason is that the company did not, or was not able to decide what products would be ready to show or should be shown. Yet another reason is that on rare occassions the product to be shown is so interesting and significant that it has to be kept under wraps until its unveiling, in this case at a show.

NEWS RELEASE

HYDRO PRODUCTS
division of Dillingham Corporation

For immediate release

HYDRO PRODUCTS ANNOUNCES NEW PRODUCTS AT MTS

In June of 1967, Dillingham Corporation acquired the Oceanographic Engineering Corporation and its product engineering and marketing aim – Hydro Products. This was the beginning of a major investment by Dillingham into the technically oriented areas of the oceanographic market. Now, just one year later, Hydro Products is bursting at the seams. The engineering budget has doubled. Marketing efforts are expanded and manufacturing capability is increased to match. Most exciting, and of most importance to the prospective customer, are the results of this considerably increased activity.

At the Fourth Annual MTS Conference and Exhibit, Hydro Products announces some twenty (20) new oceanographic instruments and accessories. The 400 sq. ft. booth displays only new products not available last year. This accomplishment is fantastic in light of the present economic factors affecting the oceanographic research market. While most manufacturers of oceanographic instrumentation are retrenching, Hydro Products is vigorously proceeding to stake its claim on leadership in an oceanographic instrumentation competition scramble.

The new products list is an impressive one evolving from over a year of design and testing, and based on years of experience in engineering and application of hardware for the ocean environment. Following is a rundown of the new products being exhibited:

New Model TC150 Television Camera

New Model SC303 UTV System Control Unit

New Model L7 Underwater Lights

New Model L8 Diver-Held Lights

New Model LP111 Incandescent Light Power Supply

All-New Photographic Line:

Model PC775 Diver-Held 70 mm Camera

P.O. BOX 2528 · SAN DIEGO, CALIFORNIA 92112 · TEL. (714) 453 · 2345 TWX (910) 322 · 1133 · CABLE ADDRESS, HYDROPROD · 11803 SORRENTO VALLEY RD.
-1-   MORE

Figure 10-2. Release for a show.

If, for whatever reasons, it is decided to go ahead with publicity work during the show, several things can be done. A press release with a photo and background information should be prepared in advance and placed in the pressroom at the show. This information should also be mailed to interested publications just before or during the show. Figure 10-2 is an example of a press release written especially for a show.

The individual responsible for press relations at the show should be contacted. He might be helpful in arranging press contacts, since he probably knows the appropriate editors and writers and knows the show's press relations opportunities and problems. Every effort should be made to contact and brief press representatives. A hospitality room should be opened, and editors and writers invited to meet, and interview if appropriate, the executives and experts available. If a product is being promoted, it should be available to look at and, if possible, to operate.

If the product cannot be operated, or if what is being promoted is a service, or if the product is too big or in an inappropriate form for showing, a movie may be in order. This can be shown during a press conference or at regular intervals according to a schedule which is posted and handed out.

COMPANY PUBLICATIONS

Some companies find that an external company publication is a justifiable expense. Its value is greater when it is part of an integrated external communications program. Information developed for other uses such as press releases, feature article material, and signed articles is usually used in company publications. Conversely, material developed for a company publication may lend itself to other uses.

Company characteristics that determine the nature of company publications are extent of diversification, technological content of products, breadth of application of products, and makeup of sales and distributor organizations.

An example of a company publication is shown in Figure 10-3. It was published by the Hydro Products Division of Dillingham Corporation. This issue was 12 pages in length, and contained 12 news or special-interest items on topics certain to appeal to the oceanographic community. These items were not about Dillingham and did not mention the company's name. The information about the company that it did contain included 14 items on Dillingham products, a story on Dillingham's Hydro Products capabilities, an item on the company's exhibit at a forthcoming society meeting, and a literature announcement.

NEWS OF OCEANOGRAPHY AND LIMNOLOGY

published by HYDRO PRODUCTS division of Dillingham Corporation

VOL. 3 NO. 4   SAN DIEGO, CALIFORNIA   JUNE 1968

FIRST DEEP CORING OF SEA FLOOR BEGINS

Dr. Maurice Ewing, left, and Dr. J. Lamar Worzel, Director and Associate Director, respectively, of Columbia University's Lamont Geological Observatory, will be Co-Chief Scientists on the first leg of the Deep Sea Drilling Project, scheduled to commence in late June.

Two of the nation's foremost geophysicists, Dr. Maurice Ewing and Dr. J. Lamar Worzel, have been named Co-Chief Scientists on the first leg of the Deep Sea Drilling Project in the Atlantic Ocean, scheduled to begin this month. The first leg will be from Orange, Texas, to New York City.

Professor Ewing is Director and Professor Worzel Associate Director of Columbia University's Lamont Geological Observatory.

JOIDES (Joint Oceanographic Institutions' Deep Earth Sampling), a deep-sea drilling and research program for determining the age and processes of development of the ocean basins, "should either confirm the hypothesis of ocean floor spreading, or

Thrusters in stern and bow of GLOMAR CHALLENGER are computer-controlled for holding ship on station during drilling of core holes.

Continued on page 4

DOWB READY FOR OPERATION

Six-mode manipulator on bow of DOWB (Deep Ocean Work Boat) is under surveillance of crew by means of Hydro Products closed circuit television for precise positioning and retrieval of objects. The camera is shown behind the vertical line.

Operational status is expected this month for DOWB, a two-man deep ocean work boat designed and built by General Motors' AC Electronics-Defense Research Laboratories for operation to depths of 6,500 feet.

The deep ocean work boat is 17 feet long and 8 ½ feet wide. It will have a 2-man life support endurance of 65 hours and a range of 26 miles.

Mounted on the DOWB is a continuously operating sonic beacon, a device which will keep the surface ship informed of the submersible's position at all times. This safety feature also will provide tracking information. An underwater sonic telephone permits contact with the mother ship on the surface.

Exclusive with DOWB is a TV viewing system with TC100 Hydro Products camera mounted on the manipulator. This rugged, highly dexterous prosthetic arm has a reach of 49 inches and a freedom of action necessary to perform useful work. The TV viewing feature will allow precision control of the prosthetic device when performing delicate operations or lifting objects. The device will lift objects weighing up to 50 pounds.

Other GM innovations include a four-motor alternat-

Continued on page 3

1

Figure 10-3.   Company publication.

152

This issue of the *Seahorse* was prepared professionally with excellent writing and photos. It even included a tear-out card a reader could send in for more information on the company's products. A two-column format was used throughout and the size was $7 \times 9\ 1/2$ inches.

Purpose

The purpose of an external company publication is simply to inform its audiences, usually customers, about the company's progress and capabilities. It strives to improve acceptance of products and services.

Standards

Since a company publication is to an extent automatically suspect in the eyes of its readers, and since business publications compete for the time of its readers, the company publication has to have very high standards in its choice of subject matter, manner of presentation, and appearance. It is extremely inportant that the subject matter and the way it is put across be relevant to the needs of the readers.

Format

Company publications range all the way from small-format, four-page newsletters to larger-than-normal, thick, four-color extravaganzas. The better ones are characterized by high-quality writing, photos, and printing. Most are near the conventional size of $8\ 1/2 \times 11$ inches, which readers generally prefer. However, smaller sizes are less expensive and the loss of effectiveness is not disastrous.

Temporary Company Publications

Some company publications, such as Westinghouse's *Engineer* and Hughes' *Vector*, have been around for many years. However, these and a few other old timers are the exception. More company publications than any other kind are started and then suspended.

Some publications are justifiably short-lived, because they are begun for a specific need and suspended when that need is pase.

One aerospace company started a standard-size, four-page newsletter which for all intents and purposes was an employee publication. Editorially excellent, its content seemed to be aimed high for an employee publication which has to have "lowest common denominator" standards. The publication was not aimed at employees, however, although they certainly received it. It was aimed at a carefully built mailing list of military officers and government civilian employees. The objective was to inform these key people about the abilities of the company to turn in an excellent performance, on time and within cost requirements, on a huge contract the company hoped to win.

OFF-THE-RECORD INFORMATION

Off-the-record information is probably given to editors and writers more often than publicity men care to admit. It is sometimes deliberately used when it is important to put some information into print but equally important that the source not be revealed. This may result in stories that attribute information to such things as informed sources or industry spokesmen.

At times, off-the-record information is simply a straightforward attempt by publicity men to give their press contacts honest answers. One reason this works is that newsmen and editors protect their sources. There is considerable justification for this in that press representatives trust publicity men who are honest with them even when it hurts. When a trusted publicity man goes to his press contacts with a story, they tend to consider it a legitimate news item and generally agree to run the story.

RESPONSES TO INQUIRIES

This is in a sense a passive form of information transferral, since the initiative is left to the publication. In many cases, companies respond poorly and sometimes not at all to press inquires. If inquiries are quickly and fully answered, publications can do justice to the company's position or capability. If inquiries go to more than one company, and if one responds while its competitor does not, the accommodating company looks good and the other looks bad. The positive approach is to consider every inquiry an opportunity rather than a nuisance.

USING THE TOOLS TOGETHER

Publicity planning is covered in detail in Chapter 7 but a review may be in order here. It is essential that publicity projects be planned, which involves the familiar process of establishing communications objectives and goals. These are largely dictated by the need and the audience. The backdrop, the arena, the ambient of the communications situation has to be examined.

Finally, specific tools have to be selected, responsibilities assigned and actions scheduled.

Audiences and Tools

Figure 10-4 shows the audiences and forms of publicity information usually used to reach them. Although by no means a universal aid, it is useful in many situations. It can be extended to include not only publicity but other communications tools such as advertising and trade show exhibits.

This type of thorough attention to planning is essential for successful publicity. The history of communications is filled with ill-advised and ineffective, even harmful, projects and programs. They were mostly due to ignorance of the practice and the effects of communications, or to haste and inattention to details.

Timing

Timing in the use of the tools depends on several outside influences. They include such items as the marketing schedule for a product, availability of opportunities such as editorial space and trade shows, availability of equipment to photograph, availability and cooperation of scientists and engineers for information, availability and cooperation of executives for decisions, printing schedules, and advertising schedules.

Combination of Tools

In using the tools, an infinite variety of combinations of the forms of publicity is possible. The particular mixture to be used depends upon the objective and the ambient. However, there are some fairly standard combinations which can be used as a target.

Saturation Program without a Press Conference

The following is an example of a saturation product publicity program in which a press conference or press briefing is *not* used. A high degree of newsworthiness is assumed.

- Present a paper before a professional group. The paper as a publicity tool is especially important in the case of a high content of technology or complexity in the product or a highly specialized area. The paper can be submitted as the "outline" for a subsequent signed article.
- Distribute a press release on the paper—one designed for the news columns of the specialized publications that serve the desired audience.

	Customer Needing The Product	Buying Influences	Stock-holders	Financial Analysts	Industry Movers and Opinion Makers	Prospective Employees	General Public
Development release	X	X	X	X	X	X	X
Case history release	X	X					
New product announcement	X	X					
State-of-the business announcements			X	X	X	X	
Plant and personnel announcements	X	X	X	X	X		X
Sales literature announcements	X						
Photo-and-caption release	X	X	X	X	X	X	X
Unsigned exclusive feature	X	X				X	
Signed exclusive article	X	X				X	
Background information	X	X					

Figure 10-4 Audiences and the forms used primarily to reach them. Background information is primarily aimed at the editors and writers to enable them to provide complete and accurate coverage. For maximum effectiveness, however, it should also be directed at the ultimate audiences.

- Offer first-use-exclusive background information to the number-one publication in the field as the basis for a product feature. This publication should be informed that a distribution of a press release is planned to coincide with the appearance of the feature.
- Distribute a press-release-length version of the product information to all other publications potentially interested.
- Reprint and mail the published product feature to customers and supply it to salesmen.
- Advertising and sales promotion is initiated at this point, and sales literature must be available.
- Issue a sales literature announcement release.
- Have an exclusive signed article published on application of the product. Since the lead time for publication of an article is a minimum of several months, it must be initiated about the same time as the earlier background information.
- Reprint the application article, mail it to customers, and supply it to salesmen.
- Enter the product in a trade show or other exhibit, and issue a press release announcing the showing. This should be sent out at least 2 months prior to the editorial closing date of the key publications in the field.
- Issue a gimmick, funny, or milestone press release. This may be based on a manufactured event.

Saturation Program with a Press Conference

When a press conference or briefing is used, the ideal combination would be something like the following.

- Conduct a press conference or press briefing. The press kit should include a news release and background information. It is usually a good idea to supply press kit information a few days in advance to business publication editors scheduled to take part in the press event. The press release should also be mailed at the time of the press event to possibly interested publications, whether or not they are invited to take part in the press event.
- Initiate advertising and sales promotion activities and have sales literature available.
- Reprint a major feature published as a result of the press conference; mail it to customers and supply it to salesmen.
- Have a signed exclusive article on application of the product published.

- Reprint the signed article; mail it to customers and supply it to salesmen.
- Issue a literature announcement release.
- Show the product at a trade show or other exhibit.
- Enter the product in a trade show or other exhibit, and issue a press release announcing the showing.
- Issue a gimmick, funny, or milestone press release.

Including International Publicity

Most companies do business overseas these days. The tools of publicity can, with a few variations, be used on the international scene in much the same way they are domestically.

The following report on an actual program illustrates the use of releases, articles, a company magazine, and international distribution.

The subject of the ABCD electrical system first appeared as a planned news release on a 1966 information program for the XYZ Company. The news release was distributed in July 1966. The subject then appeared on the 1967 program as an article subject. Information for an article was made available by XYZ engineers late in 1967. Both a long article and a short one were developed. The short one was published by an oceanographic magazine in July 1968. The long version appeared in the March 1969 issue of the XYZ company magazine. After the company magazine article was published, the long version of the article was submitted to several publications overseas. Several usages of the article in overseas publications resulted.

Special Programs

One important type of special program frequently used involves the building of an identity for an individual as an industry spokesman, or as a nationally known leader or opinion maker in a particular field. The means used include personal appearances, press releases, signed articles, papers, and speeches. Some or most of the ideas in these forms of information may be the spokesman's but the items themselves are ghostwritten. The most-used methods are probably the speech, and associated forms of communications such as press releases.

In using speeches as a means to build a reputation for an individual, it is important to keep in mind the meaning behind Edward L. Bernay's rule of not giving more than two speeches a year. One way of looking at what he was saying is that it is possible to overexpose an individual, and that it is necessary for speeches to bring out something important.

Another type of special programs involves supporting the communications effort of a major customers.

A company won a hard-fought contract to supply a huge amount of equipment for a large-scale real estate venture with the possibility of more sales later on if the venture caught on and expanded. To help the venture succeed, the company offered to help publicize it. A publicity man was assigned to do whatever was necessary to fulfill the offer. The company decided that the stratagem required was to emphasize the venture, not necessarily their product. The publicity man developed a program including background information on the venture and a series of consumer-oriented progress milestone releases. Another feature of the program was a continuing effort to place feature articles in trade and business publications. A final ingredient of the program was a series of speeches by the real estate tycoon which were written and publicized by the company's publicity man.

Yet another type of special program may help a customer keep a job or contract sold. One example is the case of a primary supplier to a contractor developing a major military or aerospace system such as a fighter plane or a spacecraft. Another example is a company doing urban work supported by a federal contract and dependent upon renewal of the contract for continuation of the work. In the latter case, the objective would be to help the federal agency administering the contract to keep the program alive.

The converse of the foregoing special program might involve enlisting the help of suppliers in publicizing a major system or project.

Smaller companies should not automatically assume that the electronic media are out of the question for them. It is true that in most cases they are not the proper media to convey the message. However, if the company is selling something very specialized, it may be useful to consider radio and television in special geographic areas. For example, if the company were in the business of supplying a new plastic liner to protect harbor pilings from marine worms, all harbor cities would be potential markets. The company might supply tapes and film clips to radio and television stations, which would catch the eyes and ears of the city fathers and harbor engineers.

11

PUBLICITY WRITING CONSIDERATIONS AND TECHNIQUES

Producing material that is published, and also gets its message across, is an essential part of the publicity process. There is no point in putting out information that is not used. Publications do not automatically snap up everything they receive. On the contrary, they use only a fraction of the material. The amount is too great, and much of what comes to them is useless and would not be run even if space were available. It may be of interest to see how one editor selects releases for his weekly business publication:

> On Thursday, which is the editorial closing day for the magazine, I put the past week's accumulation of press releases in a pile on my desk and put a wastebasket next to my chair. I pick up a release from the pile and scan it as I pass if from the pile over the wastebasket. If I haven't found anything of interest by the time I get it over the wastebasket, I drop the release and turn back to the pile. From the entire pile, which runs from a few inches to a foot high, I usually keep only a few. And not all those I keep actually get into print. I file many of them for background information for one reason or another.

To be used, publicity material must meet the needs of the publications it is aimed at, and must be presented in a way that will catch the attention of busy editors. It must be properly written and illustrated, adequately reproduced, and accurately targeted.

PREWRITING CONSIDERATIONS

Before beginning the actual production of material, a publicity writer must set boundaries for himself. This is done by using the opportunities and limitations that become apparent in thinking through the subject, the audience, the media, and the forms of publicity. Although all these are explained separately (the forms of publicity are covered in Chapters 9 and 10), they are closely related and must in practice be considered together. There are numerous elements which must be traded off against each other in such considerations.

Thinking about a subject, an audience, and media, and relating them in terms of conveying a message, results in a particular type of interaction. This leads to development of a focus or a perspective perhaps best described by the phrase "putting it all together."

Objectives

A good place to start with prewriting considerations is the subject. For effective publicity this must be an outgrowth of an objective. Producing publicity for its own sake is not generally in keeping with the way industry does things. The exception to this is when the objective is simply to help build stature or image or reputation. Even in this case, the manpower and money are usually not available to cover all the territory, and priorities must be established. This comes back around to the idea of objectives. Without the focus and discipline of practical objectives, the publicity man often skims off the most obvious and easiest, not necessarily the most useful, stories from the numerous possibilities that exist for any organization.

Subject

Wherever possible, the objective, and therefore the subject, should have strategic or long-range importance as well as tactical and immediate usefulness. This is in keeping with the idea, brought out in Chapter 7, of beginning with a strategic plan which serves as an umbrella for specific publicity plans and projects.

The idea of a message or theme is tied in with the subject. Most of the time, the message grows very neatly out of the objective. When it does not, it is usually because the objective was not clearly defined and defined in terms of publicity.

The message must be considered in light of what is newsworthy about the subject. Newsworthiness is the most serious limitation of publicity. Although it is sometimes difficult, a peg or slant can usually be found that is interesting to at least one important publication.

What all this boils down to is that, for effective publicity, the subjects of particular stories must be the result of a three-way correlation of the objective, the message, and what is newsworthy about the subject.

Newsworthiness is a very important consideration. Occasionally, however, it may be necessary or expeditious to send out information on a subject that is not newsworthy. Such a situation may occur for a variety of reasons. The most common reason is that the product or service is so mundane, uninteresting, or taken for granted that any information on it receives a minimum of attention. Even so, it may be useful to disseminate the information. One expert feels this way about it:

I've seen situations where a release got virtually no coverage. It may have been picked up by one or two books but on the whole, it bombed. It was not the writing or the handling but simply that the subject was so dull and ordinary. But despite the low level of pickup, it still was a good idea to put the story out. In a number of such cases, I've had editors contact me later in regard to something they were doing in the general area covered by the release that died. This type of release often winds up in a file of background information. The editor can't see his way clear to run the information in his news column but at the same time sees some value in it. Such information is frequently used in something like a roundup article and if it hadn't been for the release in his file, the editor might not have known we are in the business.

It is important to note that newsworthiness and timeliness are not the same thing. Timeliness is a factor in newsworthiness, but its importance varies. In the case of a daily newspaper it is highly important; to business publications, it is usually of less importance.

Audience

Another prewriting consideration is the audience. There is an old philosophical question: If a tree falls in the forest and there is no one around to hear the sound, is the sound real? In the practical world of industrial communications, if a sound is made and no one hears it, the sound does not exist. Put another way, if a message is transmitted but is not heard, then it might as well not exist, and the time, money, and effort that went into preparing it were wasted.

The reasons why messages are not heard are many. The main one is that the message becomes lost in the throng of messages aimed at a particular receiver because the sender is not well attuned to the receiver's requirements. The sender consequently does not structure or code the message in a way that can be detected and decoded by the receiver.

For the sender to know what the receivers—the audience—can and will be receptive to, he must determine the makeup and the needs of his audience. This means analyzing to some degree the background, interests, work, goals, attitudes, and prejudices of the individuals that make up the audience. Obviously, it is not possible to do this in great detail. However, the accuracy with which the audience is defined strongly affects how well the ideas will ultimately be transferred from the written page to the reader's mind.

One approach which brings a lot of insight into the nature and requirements of an audience is to consider it in terms of interest stimulation, motivation, and language.

The first thing a message must do is to interest its recipients. Beyond that, if it is to be of use to anyone, it must influence readers to act some time in the near or distant future. If there is no potential of moving readers to action, there is no use in even initiating the communications project.

In analyzing the readers of business publications, it is often pointed out that they are a captive audience. This is true to a limited extent, but it is a mistake to assume that these readers automatically read everything that might be relevant to their work. In the first place, they, like everyone else, tend to read what interests them personally, not necessarily professionally. In addition, they are literally flooded with things to read. Not only does a variety of business publications cross their desks, but there are other publications of various kinds, direct mail items from manufacturers and suppliers in the field, and a plethora of in-company material regularly sent or routed to everyone of any importance in a company.

It is a good idea, then, to assume that the audience is not a captive one. Even if it is assumed that the professional and personal interests of the audience coincide, the need to interest them still applies. One reason is, as pointed out above, that there is so much other material they must read, which competes for their attention. Another is that even scientists and engineers respond to the emotional content of what they read. For example, the idea of elegance in scientific theory is a more-or-less emotional thing. The affinity of scientists for elegant theories reaches into the domain of aesthetics. On a more practical level, there are fashions in science, engineering, and management, just as there are in other areas of endeavor. After Sputnick, space became the lodestone. Oceanography became a focal point of interest for a while. Many other areas such as microcircuitry, lasers, and computers have been or are fashionable subjects. The interest of the technical and industrial communities tends to ebb and flow in subjects such as these. This interest has a certain emotional content.

It would be absurd to suggest that industrial publicity should have a raw emotional content such as the appeal to basic human drives used in selling consumer products. It should primarily appeal to reason and experience. Nevertheless, the producers of publicity sometimes fail to take into account the emotional side of people, and thereby lose their audience before they have a chance to appeal to their reason and experience.

One way of looking at the role of emotion in communication is from the viewpoint of identification. People tend to identify with things that touch them in some way. On the rational or conscious level, the things that affect people are those that have to do with their day-to-day affairs. Such things as shopping lists, school lunch menus, bowling leagues, and bridge parties are of day-to-day interest to the housewife. Production schedules, financial reports, contracts, and research data are typical day-to-day interests of industrial people. They do not, however, identify only with these day-to-day things. There are many things that affect them on the nonrational, unconscious level. More importantly, although decisions are undertaken and considered on the conscious level, they are usually made on the unconscious or subconscious or intuitive level.

There is another element of identification that comes into play. People tend to identify more with suggestions or ideas that imply some action than with those that do not. Since they cannot possibly learn and figure out everything for themselves, people look to various authorities for guidance. They want, and more to the point, they need, to be told what to do in many aspects of their life. They are, in a word, looking to be motivated. The element of motivation is infrequently a problem in industrial publicity because it usually calls for some action (again, in its simplest form, "buy this product"). In cases in which a call to action is not inherent, however, it is important for the publicity writer to remember that he or she does not have to be reluctant to state or imply action, because that is the way people prefer it.

Yet another important item of concern in relation to the audience is that of language or specialized vocabularies. Just about every field or discipline has its own specialized vocabulary. If the audience is highly specialized in one narrow field, and if the publications that serve the field are equally specialized, then the highly specialized vocabulary of that field can be used in publicity. This is seldom the case, however, and most publicity writing must be generalized to some degree.

In the case of overlapping but similar audiences, they may have a less specialized but still technical vocabulary in common. For example, the fields of optics and electronics have come together in the specialization of electrooptics. As a result, a specialized vocabulary in electrooptics has been developed, but beyond that the physicists in the optics field and electronics engineers have had to learn how to understand each other. They both have had to generalize to an extent when talking to each other, and a more general vocabulary has evolved.

If the audience includes several diverse specializations, a great deal of interpretation and generalization must be done. However, it is almost never necessary to generalize industrial publicity to a mass media level. This is where once again a judgment factor enters. The writer must have done his homework and become acquainted with his audience to the extent that he can judge how much interpretation and generalization must be done. As Flesch suggests, "Never mind writing what the public wants—or what you suppose the public wants. Study your audience and then write what you want to say in the *form* that is most likely to appeal to them."

The following report may serve to illustrate the importance of language in industrial communications.

I was present at a briefing on a method of using certain electrical measurements to determine the geological makeup of a segment of the earth's crust. The research project in which the technique had been developed had brought together two very different types of individuals. One was a highly practical person, a mining engineer. The other was a theoretical physicist. The physicist had previously been working on the why and how of propagation of low frequency radio waves for world-wide military communications. He was interested in the effect of the earth's crust on radio waves from the viewpoint of how well the earth conducted the electrical energy. He was concerned with the property of *conductivity*. On the other hand, the mining engineer was concerned with what the way electrical energy acted told him about the nature of the earth's crust. Due to the way such things were usually measured in the mining industry, he thought in terms of *resistivity*. In a practical sense, conductivity and resistivity are the opposite of each other. Mathematically, one is the reciprocal of the other and they are expressed in different units. If conductivity is C and resistivity is R, their mathematical relationship is $C = 1/R$. Both men were talking about the same method of measurement but from clearly different viewpoints. Since both were contributing in a give-and-take session, it quickly became apparent to both that they had to get together. They agreed, happily on the basis of their audience, to talk in terms of resistivity. The rest of the session proceeded more smoothly even though the scientist had to pause occasionally when giving numbers to convert in his mind from conductivity to resistivity.

Media

The third main writing consideration is the media. For industrial publicity, this means primarily business publications. The determination of the right media for a particular publicity project is made mainly on the basis of the audience to be reached, but also on the basis of the subject. The mechanics of media selection are covered in Chapter 8.

The entire process would be simplified if the media could be selected on the basis of audience alone. This is possible with advertising since the space is purchased, and a company can say just about anything it wants to in an ad. But for publicity information to be used by a publication, it must attract the interest of an editor and must be of some immediate use to his readers. So it turns out that the main writing consideration is regard to the media is editors.

Editors are in a sense information filters, except that they are not passive. They act upon and react to information. In doing so, they use their experience and knowledge of what their readers want to read and need to know. They have certain requirements that the industrial publicity writer must keep in mind.

The foremost editorial requirement is newsworthiness. As indicated in the earlier section dealing with the element of subject, this is the most serious limitation of publicity. The publicity writer must compare the elements of his subject to the subject requirements of the publications that reach the desired audience. This can occasionally be an insurmountable problem, and the company must look to other means of communication to tell the story. In the vast majority of cases, however, it is possible to find a news slant or peg.

Closely related to newsworthiness is the idea of usefulness. Material that is useful to an editor takes one of two forms. The first is what might be called business material which is related to factors that affect buying and selling. This might include such things as financial information and market forecasting. The second form can be called technology information, and is concerned with such things as research, designing, and manufacturing. Business publications usually use both forms in varying proportions. The editor decides on the basis of his knowledge about his readers what mixture to use.

Another requirement editors have is that they need guidance. (This does not mean that they are willing to be led. On the contrary, they have a sure sense that tells them when someone is trying to use them.) Since they are not, and cannot be, fully acquainted with everything that is going on in their industry, they need some interpretation, some clues as to the meaning behind events. They are very appreciative of guidance.

Another thing about editors is that they are usually kept very busy and are often inundated with information, much of its useless. They appreciate directness, straightforwardness, and a businesslike approach in material they receive. The more direct the writing is, the faster they can tell if it is of use to them. Stories with the important facts buried in them exasperate editors. This points up the importance of the opening of any piece of writing, a subject that is dealt with in detail in the following section on writing.

WRITING CONSIDERATIONS

The aim of most writing is to transfer facts and concepts from one mind to another. Publicity writing is a special type of communication which presents concepts and facts to inform or motivate.

Hundreds, even thousands, of books and articles have been written on the subject of how to communicate in writing. What follows is an attempt to relate some methods and approaches to the specialized area of publicity writing.

It is widely thought that writing, and for that matter any form of communication, is a mysterious process, and that doing it right is the secret of the high priests of language, professional writers and teachers of writing. This is not the case. Writing is simply another human skill which can be learned. Of course, as with other human skills, different people have different aptitudes for and feelings toward writing. Still, it can be learned, and is no more mysterious than the multitude of human processes people go through every day.

One of the important characteristics of the publicity writer is that he is a craftsman who must above all be concerned with communicating with an audience. He is not an artist who writes only for himself as a form of self-expression.

The process of communicating with an audience of course goes beyond just the concern of disseminating information. It also must take into account all the things that influence the reception and understanding of the message. This means that the publicity writer must adopt a kind of egoless attitude, and must put himself firmly in the shoes of his audience. As Flesch has said, "What it amounts to is that everything you write has to be slanted toward your audience."

Beginning writers, or professionals who are not writers by occupation but must write for one reason or another, often worry excessively about grammar, punctuation, spelling, and style—the elements of composition. These elements are, however, not so awesome when seen from the viewpoint of their function which is simply to make sure that the writing is understandable. The meaning of the facts presented and ideas expressed must be clear and not ambiguous. It does not take a total knowledge of the rules and elements of composition to be able to write effectively. Frank Tripp, one-time chairman and general manager of the Gannet chain of newspapers and a writer himself, once said, "I use simple words because I can't spell the big ones. The only punctuation mark I know for sure is the period. So when I know I should make a mark of some kind I make a period and start a new sentence."

Sometimes, it's advantageous to use the easy way out illustrated in the following comment.

> I was trained as a writer and have been writing for years. Even so, I often run into language or grammar problems. Sometimes, I'll be conscientious and stop to look up the rule. More often, I find myself simply writing around the problem. For example, if it's a problem in sentence structure, I'll reorganize the sentence in a way I'm sure is right.

Working around the rules is not the same as ignoring them. Along this line, William Strunk said in *Elements of Style*, "It is an old observation that the best writers sometimes disregard the rules of rhetoric. When they do, however, the reader will usually find in the sentence some compensating merit, attained at a cost of the violation. Unless he is certain of doing as well, he will probably do best to follow the rules."

That Strunk's comment centers upon the sentence points up its importance. It is the basic and single most significant unit of writing. In its simplest form, it is a group of words which begins with a capital letter, has a subject (what the sentence is about), a predicate (what is being, was, or will be done to or by the subject), and ends with a period.

Sentences should be as short as possible, but long enough to express the thought clearly. Simple words and a straightforward way of saying things should be used. The active voice (I found that . . .) is without a doubt better than the passive (It was found that . . .) for easier reading and better understanding, but cannot often be used. Most business publications use the passive, and so do most scientists and engineers. Almost without exception, technical and specialized literature has always used the passive voice. It is probably more a matter of tradition than preference but, whatever the reason, it is a practical reality.

The end of a sentence is the last part read, and so the emphasis should be placed there. The reader tends to remember better what is important about the sentence if the emphasis is at the end. Here are some of the do's and don't's of sentence writing.

Do	Don't
Use words that will be familiar to the audience you are trying to reach	Use unfamiliar spellings or strange words The reader's eyes will skip over them
Use short and simple words whenever possible	Use long words unless a short one just will not do. But keep in mind that the shorter word is not always simplest (example: utility versus usefulness)

Use active, live words	Use inactive and dead words
Watch for jargon which may creep into your writing	Use jargon unless saying it in everyday language would overcomplicate it or insult the intelligence of the reader
Use direct statements	Use say-nothing words and unnecessary introductory and conjunctive words
Keep the number of ideas per sentence low	Try to cover too much ground in one sentence
Keep the tone positive	Use weasel words
Always use words that are concrete and specific	Use abstract words unless it is absolutely necessary

The distinction between concrete and abstract words is a consideration useful in the writing of sentences. Professionals and specialists who are not writers tend to use many abstract words. They are used to taking shortcuts in their thinking by hopping from one generalization to another without pursuing each generalization from the abstract to the concrete level. Such generalizations in writing are, however, often a block to communication, because readers do not all have the same common sets of attitudes, interests, and collections of abstractions they use for thinking. So the writer must try to make abstractions concrete wherever it is necessary. This cannot always be done, and when it cannot the abstractions should be put in a concrete framework to the extent possible. Flesch suggests: "As a rule, you should never stay at the abstract level for long; as soon as you get there, turn around and plunge again into the down-to-earth world of people and things. This 'up-and-down' writing is the only protection against misunderstanding. It is no guarantee; but it's the best method there is."

Sometimes the only way to make an abstraction specific is by using an analogy. This means likening the abstraction to something the reader knows about. For example, voltage is an abstraction which is sometimes likened to the pressure of water in a municipal supply system. The analogy is intended to create understanding by showing the way the abstraction is like something that the reader already understands. One shortcoming of the analogy is that it oversimplifies. Also, people tend to assume that, because things are alike in certain respects, they are alike in others.

Again, in Flesch's words, "What it amounts to is that everything you write has to be slanted toward your audience." Industrial publicity must finally be the result of a compromise between the need for precision and the necessity for understanding. As James Thurber said, "A word to the wise is not sufficient if it doesn't make sense."

Readability and clarity in writing have been the subject of millions of words written to help the cause of understanding in communication. One way of looking at readability and clarity in writing is from the viewpoint of simplicity. In *How to Write and Speak Effective English,* Edward Frank Allen says, "Simplicity spells the difference between ineffective and effective writing." He continues, "Paradoxically, the achievement of simplicity is not simple." Finally, he offers some suggestions on keeping writing simple. "If you would write effectively, use the simplest terms. Do not use hackneyed phrases; do not employ overworked quotations; do not be squeamish, or afraid of simple words; in short, do not try to be fancy. The reader will be grateful to you for having saved him the time and labor required to translate verbiage into simple English."

One approach to improve readability and gain simplicity that is often suggested is to "write like you talk." The reason for this suggestion is that it has been observed that the vast majority of people can make themselves understood far better when they talk than when they write. The obvious conclusion is that if people would only write the way they talk, they would be better understood. Unfortunately, it is not that simple, because here again, "the achievement of simplicity is not simple." Communicating by writing automatically rules out body language with conscious and unconscious gestures, cues, and voice effects which are such an important part of communicating by talking.

The trick is to make written words *appear* to be just like spoken language. Some of the things that characterize such writing are a lot of simple, colloquial, and even idiomatic words such as contractions; active voice; structuring for emphasis, such as starting a sentence with "and" or "but"; and all the rest of the simplifying devices such as short sentences, short words, and straightforward construction.

It is important to note that the simplest version is not necessarily the best. Simplicity must be achieved within the context of the makeup of the audience. What this means in practice is that conciseness or brevity must not be sacrificed for simplicity. If it is, members of the particular audience will either become impatient with the writing or will feel that their intelligence has been insulted.

Brevity is therefore another important characteristic of effective writing. Strunk described it very well when he said, "A sentence should contain no unnecessary words, a paragraph no unnecessary lines and a machine no unnecessary parts."

Methods of measuring readability have been devised. Two of the best known are those developed by Rudolf Flesch and Robert Gunning. In *News Editing,* Bruce Westley summarized these two methods very well:

Rudolf Flesch's original formula measures three things: sentence length, word difficulty, and number of personal references. It measures word difficulty on the basis of the number of prefixes or suffixes to be found in a hundred word sample.

Robert Gunning uses three criteria. They are sentence pattern, 'fog index,' and human interest. 'Fog index' he describes as a measure of the abstraction and complexity of words. He would appear to be employing roughly the same yardstick as Flesch.

Much of the writing of industrial communications is very formal, sometimes even stuffy. There are ways of livening writing without becoming cute. Some of the ways are to use figures of speech, a highly colloquial style, human interest material, direct quotation of experts, and humor.

Figures of speech are rare in business publications. There is no reason why they cannot be used as long as they fit and truly help explain. A colloquial style, human interest material, and humor are uncommon, but can also be used to good effect if not forced. Direct quotation is sometimes used.

These methods of livening writing have to be used with imagination and some skill. Otherwise, they might turn the piece of writing into tripe.

WRITING PRELIMINARIES

Research

The broad meaning of writing includes the element of research. This involves digging out the information needed to do the writing job. Industrial publicity information is obtained in one of three ways. The first is by interview. The second is by using existing information such as reports or papers. The third is through a write-up prepared especially as the basis of publicity.

For a short press release on an uncomplicated subject, it may only be necessary to read some existing information to write the story. It might entail calling an expert to verify some facts. The whole process of researching and writing might take a day of one man's time.

The more complicated a subject, and the more detailed the publicity write-up must be, the longer it takes to research and write. It could involve several hours of briefings by different experts, and many hours of reading in the research phase. Once into the writing, it may be necessary to go back to the experts to clarify points the writer missed the first time around.

Gestation

After research, the writer should make every effort to let the information percolate through his thought processes. Most writers feel this gestation period is absolutely essential, especially when the subject is complicated and the write-up is to be lengthy.

An outline should be made during the gestation period. Experienced writers can often outline short pieces on uncomplicated or familiar subjects in their heads, often while they are researching. Most newspaper reporters can do this. But even an experienced writer needs to outline long pieces on complicated or unfamiliar subjects.

An outline helps the writer to straighten out his thoughts and to cull irrelevant ideas and facts. Decisions as to what is or is not relevant are made by relating the information to the objective and the audience. So the outline, the skeleton of the story, must fit into a framework formed by the objective and the audience.

The gestation period gives the writer a chance to sort out the ideas and build the structure. There must be time for the writer's involuntary thought and memory processes to function in the back room of his mind. There is no better way to put the story concept and framework in order. Some writers are able to handle bigger chunks of a subject area at a time, and some can more quickly structure their thinking than others, but gestation is always part of the process. In the vast majority of cases, if this time is not allowed, time is wasted later because of false starts, rewriting to eliminate irrelevant material, and reorganizing.

There is another reason for the gestation period. Even if the writer is an expert on his subject, his first impulses concerning what to put on paper are usually wrong. That is because they are almost always what is cute, naive, or trite about the subject. It takes time for the writer's mind to compare, run through, and select from his experiences so as to acquire a deeper meaning of the subject.

Outlining

To return to the outline, it can be either topical or expository in form. A topical outline is an itemized breakdown like the one taught in English composition. An expository outline is a sort of pre-summary or -synopsis of the story. Sometimes it is useful to use both approaches, especially if the subject is complicated. Each form has its advantages. The topical outline gives a better idea as to how the story should be structured, and the expository outline better defines the message or concept to be discussed. Some writers become so adept at defining the message in an expository outline that it can be used as the basis of the opening of the story.

PRODUCING COPY

If the preliminary steps of research, gestation, and outlining are done with a measure of care, the writing part should be easier than it is usually thought to be. There is no question that it is work, and in some cases very hard work. But with adequate preparation, some careful thought along the way, and attention to detail, writing can proceed smoothly and systematically to its conclusion.

By the time the writing actually begins, the writer should have a thorough understanding of the subject. No matter how technical the subject matter, it is possible for a writer to gain enough working knowledge about the subject to explain it in terms his readers can understand. Lincoln Barnett, a journalist, wrote a book which clearly explained Albert Einstein's theories. Einstein himself said, "Lincoln Barnett's book represents a valuable contribution to popular scientific writing." The book is entitled *The Universe and Dr. Einstein*, and is an expansion of an article by Barnett which appeared in *Harper's* magazine. Another instance is the books by Robert Ardrey entitled *African Genesis* and *The Territorial Imperative*. Ardrey, a playwright and journalist, learned enough about anthropology to write two books which have been quoted by practicing anthropologists.

One of the reasons it is necessary for the writer to understand his subject is so that he will be able to strip it down into its component parts or bare essentials. One of the best ways of explaining a subject is to relate the essentials to items of experience the writer knows his readers have.

It is important for the writer to try not to be literary or journalistic. He should try to use what works for him in the simplest way, with as much clarity as possible. Initially, the important thing is to put as much as possible on paper. Edward Frank Allen suggests:

Write as fast as thoughts come into your mind. The principal object is to transfer your ideas to paper. As you write, observe all the rules of grammar and syntax that come to your mind instinctively. Then, having written, go back and make those corrections which may be necessary on second thought. You will discover that the more you write (provided, of course, you take care not to perpetrate your errors), the more such rules will occur to you instinctively, without conscious effort, as though by second nature.

Another thing to keep in mind during the writing process is the degree of interpretation and explanation decided upon in the prewriting consideration of the subject and the audience. Again, if the makeup of the audience is highly specialized, and if the subject area is a familiar one to both editors and audience, less interpretation is needed. Toward the other end of the scale, where you find a less specialized audience and less familiarity with a subject, more interpretation is of course necessary.

It has been suggested at times that the writer should simply arrive at a lowest common denominator standard and write everything to that standard. One disadvantage of this approach is the risk of insulting the editor's and the audience's intelligence. Another is that it is more time-consuming and so reduces the writer's efficiency. Finally, the more interpreting the writer does, the more he moves toward examples and figures of speech to explain the subject. Again, the risk here is the possibility of having the story become trite.

Length is another consideration during the writing phase. The aim should be to put as much in a story as will be used by the most horizontal publication in the planned distribution. At the same time, it is important to not bury the editor or his readers in useless facts or statistics.

The Opening

The two main functions of a piece of writing are to stimulate the reader's interest, and to leave him with ideas or facts that he will remember. The opening should stimulate interest. The main way it does this is to cause questions to form in the reader's mind or, in other words, to arouse his curiosity. The reason the reader continues to read is the hope that his questions will be answered.

In addition to stimulating interest, the opening also summarizes the main idea of the piece. If it is a short write-up, such as a news release, it is especially important to put the main idea in the opening or lead. Editors or readers may not read beyond the lead.

It is important to note that the main idea of many stories prepared by publicists is buried. If the editor is interested enough, or in the right mood, he might take the time to dig out the buried main idea. It is more likely that he will not.

To make the opening interesting and to introduce the main idea, it is often necessary to spend as much time on it as in writing the entire remainder of the story. This has the side benefit of being the core of the story. The rest of it will be an amplification of the opening.

Most pieces of writing can be broken into units. These may be paragraphs or larger units. Every unit should have an opening sentence or section which summarizes the unit. This method takes a lot of time and work, which may not be warranted in all cases.

The main reason for breaking things into units is to provide for the possibility that the reader may stop at any point. This could be after the first sentence, the first paragraph, or somewhere further on. With this in mind, it is important to summarize the main idea in the opening, and then summarize subordinate ideas in much the same way in units of descending importance.

Organization

Two significantly different schemes of organization are used for short and long write-ups. Organization is more important in the case of short write-ups which in practice are almost always news releases. They need to be packaged in the best way possible.

As explained above, the first paragraph must gain the editor's (and ultimately, the reader's) attention. The succeeding units of the short write-up elaborate on and justify the opening, but still in a reasonably concise form. Thereafter, the subject of the write-up is explained in further detail if necessary. Last, nearly all short write-ups are accompanied by photos, or other illustrations, and these are explained in captions which may be attached to the photos or may be part of the write-up.

In the long write-up, usually a feature article, sometimes signed by its writer, organization is less crucial. Because editors receive fewer of them, and because they know it takes a lot of time and effort to write a long piece, editors tend to read them carefully. Under these circumstances, the subject matter, not necessarily the way it is packaged, "sells" the article.

The most common organization for a long write-up is: summary, body, and conclusions. Frequently, however, the conclusions are part of the opening summary. Sometimes, a "perspective" opening precedes the summary, and is often anecdotal in nature. The write-up therefore may have the form: anecdotal opening, summary, explanatory body. In this case, it resembles very closely the organization of the short write-up.

A manuscript for a long write-up should contain the text of the piece, a list of illustration captions, a list of references if needed, and usually reproducible illustrations. Some magazines prefer to draw their own diagrams and charts and, in that case, only legible sketches are necessary. Photos should preferably be in the form of 8 × 10-inch glossy prints.

Rewriting

The final, and an essential, part of the writing process is rewriting and revising. Samuel Johnson's admonition, although it is a safe bet that he did not have industrial publicity in mind when he said it, is appropriate. He said, "Read over your compositions, and when you meet with a passage you think is particularly fine, strike it out." Rudolf Flesch modernized and made more specific somewhat the same idea when he said, "Those words you liked so well when you wrote them will probably have to be cut in half and completely rearranged."

Most pieces of writing need to go through one or more phases of rewriting or revising. Some highly experienced writers are able to edit as they go along, and not much revising is needed when they finish. Most of the rest of us put down a lot of things in the first flush of composition that are incomprehensible to others, misspelled, ungrammatical, and awkward in structure—stuff that on the whole we would be embarrassed to see in print. Unlike a lot of things, however, writing can be worked over and redone, time after time if necessary.

An essential part of the rewriting step is to check accuracy. It is common knowledge in the newspaper business that the facts that are most likely to be wrong are those that are so obviously correct. Here is an example from one writer's experience that shows that the writer has to take it upon himself to assure correctness.

I put out a press release once that had the word "aperture" misspelled in three different places. It was my own mistake. When I wrote the story I wrote the word "aperature" in all three places; I put an extra "a" in it. I know I'm a lousy speller and I should have been more careful. In the writing and approval process, the story was typed at least three times by different secretaries. It was read for accuracy by at least three engineers, a patent attorney, three marketing men, and a half dozen managers in my company. Also, an unknown number in the customer's organization read it when we submitted it for their approval. Of course, most of these people were reading it for reasons other than checking the accuracy of the spelling but it's strange that no one caught the error. It was finally pointed out to me, to my chagrin, by an editor who called me on it. He said that it looked like it should be aperture but he wanted to check—and here he got a little sarcastic—to see if a new word had been coined.

REFERENCES

Edward Frank Allen, *How to Write and Speak Effective English*, Fawcett Publications, Inc., New York, 1959.

Rudolf Flesch, *The Art of Readable Writing*, Harper & Brothers, New York, 1949.

Robert Gunning, *The Technique of Clear Writing*, McGraw-Hill Book Company, New York, 1952.

Norman G. Shidle, *Clear Writing for Easy Reading*, McGraw-Hill Book Company, New York, 1951.

William Strunk, Jr., and E. B. White, *The Elements of Style*, The Macmillan Company, New York, 1959.

Bruce Westley, *News Editing*, Houghton Mifflin, The Riverside Press, Cambridge, Mass., 1953.

12

PRODUCING PRESS RELEASES

Chapters 9 and 10 dealt with an explanation of the forms of publicity, and Chapter 11 was concerned with the general aspects of publicity writing. This chapter is a more detailed treatment of press releases.

A majority of publicity information is disseminated through one of the forms of the press release.

Each form of the press release has characteristics of its own, but there are many features the various forms have in common. One set of common features comes under the category format.

PRESS RELEASE FORMAT ELEMENTS

The format of the press release is its framework—the elements most release have in common. These common elements are the result of practices that have evolved over the years. Most of these practices are based on good reasons, and help publications in understanding and handling releases. Where common practice actually contributes to understanding and facilitates processing, it is of course wise to follow it. As a practical matter, however, some common practices are of questionable value, and some good practices are not commonly used. What this boils down to is that the publicity man has to familiarize himself with the practices and make an independent judgment on what fits his company or client best.

The example releases in Chapter 9 show many, but by no means all, of the press release elements. The following is a breakdown of common elements.

Company Identification

Starting literally at the top, most companies use an identifying symbol or otherwise distinctive imprint for their press releases. The theory is that a familiar imprint catches an editor's attention. Since people respond more to familiar things than to strange ones, this argument has some validity. And when a familar letterhead becomes identified in an editor's mind with consistently useful information, its effectiveness is increased manyfold.

Agencies often do not use identifying imprints. Instead, they usually just type the name and address of the client company at the top of the release. The reason seems to be that they do not want editors to confuse the name or symbol of the agency with that of the client, or vice versa. This appears to be in the mutual best interest of the agency and client.

A company imprint can simply be the stationery normally used for correspondence. However, many, if not most, companies choose to have a special press release imprint designed. This imprint includes the company's symbol or name or both, and usually includes the word "news," sometimes the word "information." A sampling shows these uses:

- News Release
- ———News (the company's name in the blank)
- News from———(here also, the company's name in the blank)
- News Service
- News Bureau
- News for Release
- News Department
- Press Information

Figure 12-1 shows a representative imprint. The words "News Release" as part of the imprint are the most common. The "———News" and "News from———" follow close behind in frequency of use.

Some companies use a family of imprints with slightly different forms for different types of press releases. One company has different imprints, with a strong family resemblence of course, for types of publicity information they refer to as "news," "product news," "catalog news," and "technical papers." These different imprints are used to make it easier for editors to identify the type of information they are looking at. This is especially useful in the offices of large business publications where one editor may be assigned to handle product news, another literature announcements, and yet another the industry news columns of the publication, and so on.

Company Contact

Most press releases give the name and telephone number of a person in the company to contact for further information. These are usually placed at the top right of the release. Some of the companies that do not include a name and number omit them because they are afraid that this will invite questions

NEWS RELEASE ALUMINUM COMPANY OF AMERICA · 1501 ALCOA BUILDING
PITTSBURGH, PA 15219

Editorial Information:	Gordon C. Meek	(412) 553-4466

FOR RELEASE AT 10 AM, EDT,
MONDAY, JULY 8, 1968

WASHINGTON, D. C., July 8 -- Oceanography ultimately could constitute
the world's biggest industry, and will be the glamor business of the 1970's if it can
attract an adequate number of investors and entrepreneurs, Chairman Frederick J.
Close of Aluminum Company of America said here today.

Describing the undeveloped potential of the seas as "The Sleeping Giant,"
Mr. Close told delegates to the Marine Technology Society's fourth annual conference and exhibit:

"The amount of progress that will be made in oceanography during the next
decade will depend on the degree of cooperation that prevails between government
and private industry."

Mr. Close said a long step toward adequate recognition of the vast potential
of oceanography was taken recently in a proposal endorsed by President Johnson for
"an International Decade of Ocean Exploration for the 1970's."

"This," Mr. Close asserted, "could indeed fulfill the hope that President
Johnson has voiced for it as 'an historic and unprecedented adventure.'"

Remarking that as recently as a week ago Alcoa had demonstrated its own
expanding interest in oceanography by announcing a multi-million-dollar program
involving the building of ALCOA SEAPROBE, the most advanced deep ocean search
and recovery ship ever planned, Mr. Close said:

CHANGE FOR THE BETTER -more- ... WITH ALCOA ALUMINUM

Figure 12-1. News release imprint.

from editors and is just asking for trouble. If an editor has a question, however, he will contact the company anyway. And the longer it takes him to reach the person in the company who will field the question, the les friendly he will feel. This may be reflected in his treatment of the story. S it is generally a good idea to include the name and number of a contact.

Release Number

Some companies number their press releases. Some large firms find it necessary to simplify filing and retrieval. A small company that issues, say, one release in a year's time does not have this problem. Still, it is generally a good idea to assign a number. If an editor inquires about the release, the number is a shortcut way of referring to it. Also, over a period of years, press releases add up. As press release subjects dim in the minds of interested parties, there may be confusion that a number could dispell.

All kinds of numbering systems are used. Some make use of the date of issue in a coded form. For example, October 24, 1972 might become 102472. Another numbering method related to date uses the year, followed by the number of the release for that year. For example, if the year is 1972 and the release is the fourth that year, the number will be 72-4.

When press releases are numbered, the number may be found in the release anywhere. However, the best place for it is at the top right, with the contact name and telephone number.

"For Use" Line

A line that gives the conditions for use of the release usually appears at the top left of the page, under the company identification and just above the beginning of the text of the release. The majority of such lines (65 percent in one sampling) say simply, "For immediate release." Some others state the information is for release on a given date; for example, "For release A.M.'s October 24, 1972." Some other releases give no conditions at all. A small minority state: "For immediate use."

The conditions line is a convention normally observed by publications. However, most editors do not hold a sensational story for several days. If the time of release is critical, then it is not a good idea to mail it in advance and rely on the publications to hold it. Instances in which timing might be critical involve such events as announcing price changes, testifying before a government committee, and filing a law suit. If it is considered essential to put information out at the same time the event is happening, messenger services and agencies can be used to distribute releases.

Headline

Most releases—75 percent in one sampling—have headlines. When they are omitted, it is often in the belief that editors prefer to write their own. This is true, and the headline a company or agency puts on a release is rarely, if ever, the one used when the story appears. Headlines are, however, useful to editors in that they summarize what the release is about. If possible, the headline should be kept to one line. If used at all in the headline, the company's name should appear at the end of the line, not the beginning. Nearly all headlines are all in capital letters. Some are underlined, but this is not really necessary.

Dateline

About half of the release in the sampling referred to above had datelines. All those with datelines used the name of a city in the dateline; half of them used the issue date of the release, in the dateline. Since some business publications use datelines, and some others have a practice of referring to the city where the subject of the story originated or happened, it is usually a good idea to include the name of a city in the form of a dateline or in some other way.

"More" Line

If the release is more than one page in length, the word "more" should be put at the bottom of all but the last page. It usually appears in the form:

—more—

If the "more" line is not included, and if the succeeding pages become lost, then the editor may not be able to tell if the pages he has are the complete release. Also, if there are no more pages, the editor has to decide whether that is the end or whether he should look for another page. Granted, it is a minor decision, but it take a finite amount of time and the editor appreciates not being forced to make it.

Spacing

The first element of spacing is the space at the top of the first page of the release. There should be enough to allow an editor to write printing or other instructions.

The text of the release should be typed with double spacing. Some companies use a space and a half in a lengthy release. Occasionally, someone issues a release that is single-spaced. This is irritating to editors. If they want to use the story and edit it for publication, single spacing allows no room to make changes within the text. If the editor has only a slight interest in a story to begin with, or is particularly rushed, he very likely will throw the release away rather than go to the trouble of working around minor problems such as single spacing.

Slug Line

The slug line in a release is placed at the top left of the second and succeeding pages for identification in case the pages become separated from the preceding ones. It should consist of key words from the headline and should be as short as possible, one word being the ideal.

Although most companies do not include slugs, they are useful to publications. In cases in which an editor uses a well-written release and just edits rather than rewrites, pages may become separated somewhere between arrival and typesetting. A slug makes it easier to find stray pages.

The slug does not replace the page number; that should be included also. It may be part of the slug or separate.

End Marks

A wide variety of marks are used to indicate the end of the story. It is wise to use some such marking for somewhat the same reasons the "more" line is used. It frees the editor from having to decide if he has reached the end or if there is more to follow.

The most common end mark is the # sign. Next in frequency of use is -30-. This is the mark traditionally used by newspapermen to signify the end of their copy. Another mark frequently used is -0-.

Other marks used include "end," asterisks, coded dates, initials, $\oplus$, and even the name of the company.

Illustration Enclosure Line

Almost never used, the illustration enclosure line is very useful to publications. It follows the end mark and simply states that a photo is enclosed. It should be included even if the accompanying photo has a caption pasted to it. Again, this is for the convenience of the editorial publications staff.

Gathering and Stapling

The pages of the release should be stapled together, and should of course be in order. Multiple-page releases sometimes come to editorial offices loose.

The pages can easily become separated and lost in the mass of paper that ebbs and flows in the offices of publications.

Publicity men may send out unstapled releases because they consider it proper editorial procedure. Manuscripts for books and long articles are usually submitted loose. However, press releases are not manuscripts of that type, and business publications find it more convenient to handle stapled material.

Glossy prints should not be stapled to a release. They usually do not have margins large enough to allow room for the damaged area caused by a staple. Reproductions of line drawings usually have enough space for such a damaged area, and generally can be stapled to the release.

Length

The general rule for the length of press releases is that they should be as short as possible. But they should be long enough to satisfy the needs of whatever publication is likely to use the most information.

In the press release survey mentioned, the stories ranged from one to eight pages in length. The average length was about two pages, and the majority had between one and three pages.

Captions

Less than half the releases in the survey included illustrations. If this is typical of the situation in general, many publicity men are missing good opportunities for editorial coverage. Publications always need good photos, diagrams, and artist's conceptions.

Virtually all illustration captions are written to stand alone, to be usable apart from a press release even though they are sent out with one. The reason is that in many cases publications run just a photo with a "cut line"—a brief caption—and no separate article. Even if an article is also used, the illustration usually has a cut line that can stand on its own.

Publications sometimes use good illustrations just to break up the text and attract the attention of readers.

Captions are usually written so they can be used independent of a press release. But it can be beneficial to have some tangible link between them. One method of doing this, the illustration enclosure line, was mentioned previously. Some other methods are:

- The illustration can be referred to in the body of the release. For example, a statement such as "As shown in the accompanying photo . . ." can be included.

- Illustrations should be numbered, and the number used in an illustration enclosure line. In the case of glossy prints, the number should be stamped on the back or written so it does not damage the print (with a soft pencil or a felt-tip pen). It is also a good idea to stamp the company's name on the back of prints.
- The press release number should appear on the caption.
- The name of the company, its address, and the name and telephone number of a contact should be included, and should be the same as on the press release.

Most captions have a lead-in, again following journalistic practice. This consists of a summarizing phrase which begins the caption. In effect, it is a miniature headline. It is part of the first line of the caption, and is usually all in capital letters. Figure 12-2 is an example of a caption with such a lead-in.

If fastened to the print, the caption should be pasted with rubber cement. Tape should not be used, since it adheres too well and may pull the print apart when the caption is removed. Another alternative is special caption paper which has a rubber cement type of adhesive strip along its top. The adhesive strip is covered by paper which can be peeled off. The narrow strip along the top of the paper containing the adhesive may be perforated, so that the caption can easily be torn from the print.

Captions are usually one paragraph of several lines.

Reproduction

Most press releases are produced by Multilith or offset printing. Some are produced on office copy machines. In regard to reproduction, the important thing to remember is that, the more professional looking and the more legible the release, the better its reception. Editors see all levels of quality, in the reproduction of releases as well as in their clarity and newsworthiness. A news release that is sleazy in appearance may exasperate an editor to the point where he wastebaskets it without giving it the chance it may deserve.

A completely new reproduction method has come into limited use—the producing of releases on typing machines. This enables a company to provide an original typed copy for every editor. The original may have some effect on the reception of the release by an editor, in that it might give him the impression that he is the only one receiving the story. If the method is frequently and widely used, however, the editors will become suspicious of all originals.

Machine typing probably should not be used, because it borders on being unethical. Another disadvantage is that the cost is high, something on the order of 25¢ per copy.

Format Elements Do's and Don't's

In summary, the format elements that should be part of every press release are given in the following checklist.

- Imprint the company name and symbol, address, and some indication that it is a press release. (The exception is that agencies generally do not use an imprinted first page; they usually just give, in typewriting, their name and the name of the client company at the top of the first page.)
- List the name, address, and telephone number of someone in the company who can field questions that may result from a release. This should be placed at the top right.

Figure 12-2. Caption lead-in.

- A press release number should be given. The best place for it is below the contact name and number.
- A line should be included giving the conditions for use of the release. For example, "For immediate release" is the most common such line. It should appear at the upper left, above the place where the text of the release begins.
- A one-line headline summarizing the release, or at least giving a strong indication of what it is about, should be the first element of the text of the release. Most companies put the headline all in capital letters.
- A dateline should precede the first paragraph of the release. It should give the name of the city of origin and, if not mentioned elsewhere, the dateline should include the date the release is mailed. An alternative way of handling the dateline is to enter the city and date at the upper right, a double space below the contact name and number.
- Adequate space should be left at the top of the release and in the margins for editor's instructions.
- The text of the release should be typed double spaced for ease in editing.
- If the release is longer than one page, the word "more" should be centered on a line by itself at the bottom of the page.
- A line giving key words for the headline should appear at the top left of the second and succeeding pages of a release. Its purpose is to help identify the page if it becomes separated from the rest of the release.
- Page numbers should be included on the second and succeeding pages of a release.
- An end mark of some kind, such as a number symbol (#) or -30-, should appear at the end of the text of the release.
- If an illustration is sent along with the release, a line should be included, following the text of the release, indicating that an illustration is enclosed.
- The pages of a multiple-page release should be in order and stapled together.
- Captions should be written to be usable independently of the release.
- The release number should be referred to on any caption sheet.
- Also, the name of the company, its address, and the name and number of a contact should be included on the caption sheet.
- Illustations should be numbered; glossy prints should have the number stamped or written on the back in a manner that does not

damage the print. It is also a good idea to stamp the company's name on the back of prints.

- A caption lead-in, which is a summarizing or attention-getting phrase in caps, should begin the text of the caption.
- Captions should be pasted to prints with rubber cement.

In regard to format elements, some things to definitely *avoid* are:

- Typing a release with single spacing.
- Backing up the release; that is, typing on both sides of a page.
- Printing releases on colored paper.
- Sloppy reproduction.
- Hidden information, such as the name of a contact at the end of the release. An editor may not read that far.
- Photos without captions.
- Photos and captions with no company or agency identification.
- Taping captions to prints.
- Glossy prints smaller than 8 × 10 inches.
- Halftone photo reproductions sent along to illustrate releases.
- Fastening photos to captions with staples or paper clips.
- Retouched photos.
- Enclosure of a photo with no caption and no reference to it in the release.

WRITING PRESS RELEASES

Again, one of the background considerations in any type of writing is the audience. As pointed out in the previous chapter, in the case of publicity writing, there are actually two groups to keep in mind: the editors of business publications and their readers. What the editor needs is explained by W. R. Harrison in *Write for Trade Journals*. He says, "Fundamentally, the editor needs *facts*. The facts must be *accurate*. The facts should, if possible, point up an *idea*. The idea should preferably be *new*, since genuinely new ideas are comparatively rare. An old idea, on the other hand, should be given a new lease on life by a new or different *presentation*." Readers look to business publications for those new ideas. They want to find ways to do their jobs better.

Another background consideration, again referring to the previous chapter, is the type of writing required in the production of publicity. The material should be written simply and clearly, using as few words as possible. The number of ideas and long words per sentence and per paragraph should be kept to a minimum. Concrete rather than abstract words should be used wherever feasible.

Beyond the foregoing background considerations and the other considerations given in the preceding chapters, there are more specific considerations which apply to the writing of press releases. The two paramount ones are the type of opening—the lead—and the type of organization or structure. These two elements are closely related, in that the structure of a release is dependent upon the type of lead used.

The Lead

Virtually all press releases use one of three types of lead, the journalism, the general summary, and the perspective summary leads.

Journalism Lead. The classic journalism lead answers the questions who, what, when, where, and why. However, as W. R. Harrison points out, "in business publications, the 'why' doesn't often appear but none of the other four can be safely omitted."

Here is an example of a journalism lead from an American Mining Congress press release.

> DENVER, Colo.—Ladies attending the American Mining Congress' 1970 mining convention in Denver September 27–30 will be getting first-hand reports from experts on how the growing public concern for the environment affects themselves, their families, and the mining industry.

In this lead the "five W's" are:

- Who—the ladies attending the convention.
- What—the first-hand reports the ladies will get.
- When—September 27–30, 1970.
- Where—at the mining convention in Denver.
- Why—the mining industry's deep concern for the environment.

Another example of a journalism lead is:

> NEW YORK, N. Y., March 24—A small, accurate, reliable instrument for testing complete synchro systems will be displayed by Associated Missile Products, a division of American Machine & Foundry Company, in Booth 1512 at the 1958 National Conference of the Institute of Radio Engineers opening here today. The new tester promises to simplify greatly the isolation and correction of faults in these control systems so vital to national defense.

The "five W's" in this case are:

- Who—Associated Missile Products Company.
- What—synchro system test instrument.
- When—today (March 24, 1958).
- Where—at the 1958 National Conference of the Institute of Radio Engineers in New York City.
- Why—The why in this case is not stated, but is strongly implied. The reason the instrument was exhibited was to enable customers to see it and hopefully to stimulate sales.

General Summary Lead.   A standard general summary lead begins with a capsule summary in the form of an arresting or interesting statement, usually a one-sentence paragraph. This opening statement is normally followed by a more detailed summary paragraph. The following are three examples.

DOWNEY, Calif., April 11, 1970—A slimmed-down version of the Saturn V's second (S-II) stage rocket will make its first flight in the Apollo 13 mission.
Built by North American Rockwell's Space Division for NASA's Marshall Space Flight Center, the stage will have a launch pad unfueled weight of approximately 78,050 pounds. It is about 3000 pounds lighter than the comparably equipped and instrumented S-II for the Apollo 12 mission.

CULVER CITY, Calif., April 27—Development of a successful all-plastic missile airframe was announced today by the U.S. Air Force and Hughes Aircraft Company.
The technique entails molding chopped glass fiber-reinforced plastic into four identical missile quadrants. The four segments are then bonded together to form a complete missile airframe, said Charles G. Walance, manager of the Hughes components and materials laboratory, where the method was developed.

A new high-performance spherical instrument case, fabricated of chemically strengthened glass and capable of reaching virtually all ocean depths, has been developed by Corning Glass Works.
The 10-inch diameter housing—seen as a probable forerunner of a design for man-sized glass spheres for deep-sea exploration—has been proof-tested to 30,000 feet simulated depth and has been designed to survive 4000 cycles to 20,000 feet, Corning reported.

Perspective Summary Lead. This type of summary lead also begins with a capsule summary followed by a more detailed summary. Up to that point, the perspective summary closely resembles the general summary. Thereafter, however, the perspective summary has a section, usually one paragraph of one or two sentences, that explains a principle or interprets signifcance. Sometimes this is in the form of statements attributed to an authority in the field. The following are two examples of perspective summary leads.

HOUSTON, Tex.—A three-pound electronic device which looks like a metal cigar box is helping to protect Apollo astronauts on their missions to the moon. The metal box contains the space vehicle's nuclear particle detection system, designed and manufactured by Philco-Ford Corporation under a $1.7 million subcontract with North American Rockwell Corporation, prime spacecraft contractor for the National Aeronautics and Space Administration.
Among the hazards astronauts must face is the possibility of solar flares— eruptions on the surface of the sun—occurring while the spacecraft is in orbit. Solar flares bombard broad areas of space with radioactive alpha particles and protons.

EL SEGUNDO, Calif., June 15—A new scanning device, designed to diagnose whether the nation's resources are well or ailing, has been developed by Hughes Aircraft Comppany here and delivered for tests with NASA's Earth Resources Technology Satellite (ERTS-A), scheduled for launch next year.
An engineering model of the instrument, called a Multi-spectral Scanner (MSS), is now undergoing tests at General Electric Company's space division, Valley Forge, Pa., where the ERTS satellite is being built under direction of NASA's Goddard Space Flight Center.
The scanner is designed to detect and record the light "signature" of solar energy emitted by agricultural crops, forests and rivers to indicate their environmental health, and to pinpoint underground deposits of minerals and oil, said Tom Mattis, Hughes MSS program manager.

In both cases, the third paragraphs is the perspective section. These paragraphs explain the problems the systems are designed to solve.

The *general* summary leads given in the preceding section do not contain a perspective section. They simply give the facts. But it is necessary to include a section that interprets significance in cases in which it is not clear.

The perspective section of this type of release is followed by a detailed explanation.

Indirect Summary Lead. This form of lead begins with a brief explanation of an interesting or important event or principle. The actual subject of the release is then put in the context of the event or principle. Usually, this is an explanation of how a product or service is used at an event or to solve a problem. A detailed explanation then follows. The following is an example of the indirect summary lead.

> SPACE CENTER, HOUSTON, Tex.—Except for landing on the lunar surface, Apollo 10 is a dress rehearsal for the actual moon mission of Apollo 11.
> Instruments, equipment, techniques and procedures will be wrung out by astronauts Thomas Stafford, John Young and Eugene Cernan in preparation for the historic landing.
> One of the precision instruments aboard the Apollo 10 is the Omega wrist 4-dial chronograph. This unique timing device is the only wrist watch worn by the astronauts while flying in space. Many of the spacemen wear the watch for everyday use.

Quotations

When or when not to use quotations is often a source of confusion. In general, attributing statements made in press releases to individuals should be avoided. One reason is that most business publications do not use the names of individuals; if they quote a source at all, they usually use only the name of the company in attributing routine statements. For example, "The ABC Company said that its new valve will reduce repair time by at least 50 percent."

Another reason for not usually using quotations is that some agencies have indiscriminately attributed statements to key men in their client organization and editors have come to realize this. This was often done simply to feed a client's ego and thereby solidify the agency's position.

There are some occasions when attributed statements can or should be considered. These include: (1) When an important announcement is being made by an important individual. An example might be a stock issue announcement by the chairman of the board of directors. (2) When a well-known authority is involved, such as a world-renowned scientist. (3) When there does not seem to be a simple and telling way to describe something that may be too specialized or too abstract for a particular audience, it may be useful to attribute to an expert a general statement that explains a concept or technique in general terms without going into a detailed description that might be difficult to understand.

Press Release Structure

Inverted Pyramid.   Most press releases use a structure or organization journalists refer to as the inverted pyramid. With this structure, information is arranged in descending order of importance and increasing detail.

One reason for using the inverted pyramid is that some readers have less of an interest in, or need for, the details of a story. If the inverted pyramid is used, a reader can stop at any point and still be sure no additional significant details are given in the rest of the story. Another reason for using the inverted pyramid is to facilitate editing. A properly structured pyramid story can be cut after any paragraph and still give the essential information.

The straight inverted pyramid story is not difficult to write in the case of straightforward and uncomplicated subjects. The more specialized and complicated a subject is, however, the more difficult the inverted pyramid becomes. This can be handled to an extent by using what might be called a double inverted pyramid. This entails starting with a primary idea or statement in the first half of the lead, and then stating the secondary idea in the second half of the lead. Following that is first an elaboration of the primary idea, and then an elaboration of the secondary idea. The inverted pyramid can be extended to three ideas, but probably not beyond that. Multiple pyramiding must be skillfully handled to avoid choppiness and confusion. Besides, it is hard to rank more than two or three ideas in descending order of importance.

The examples in the preceding section, on the lead, have the inverted pyramid structure but present one concept. The following release is an example of a multiple pyramid. It presents three ideas.

HOUSTON, Tex.—Photographic technologists at Philco-Ford Corporation in Houston have perfected a color slide technique designed as a major aid to flight controllers in guiding American astronauts to a safe landing on the moon.

The color slides will make their first appearance at NASA's Mission Control Center during Apollo 10, the lunar orbital mission scheduled for May 18. The new metal-etched, glass-substrate color slide technique also is adaptable to commercial projection needs.

Technicians at Philco Houston Operations overcame problems of intense ultraviolet radiation, heat and extreme magnification in creating the first color reference slides for space flight control.

The slides contain data on the acceptable limits of performance for each mission. Stored in disk containers selected by computer signals, they are used to monitor missions from launch to splashdown. Flight controllers compare current mission information against the reference slides to judge whether or not the mission is going well.

Any spacecraft performance deviation which exceeds acceptable limits can result in attempts to fix the malfunctioning system, an abort or an early termination of the mission. Validity of the slides is tested over and over in preflight simulations of each mission before the spacecraft ever leaves the ground.

Prior to this color breakthrough a reference slide could be projected in only one color on the 10 × 20-foot screen in the Mission Operations Control Room, this color being variable by means of seven selective color filters in the projector.

Introduction of a second color to the reference slides has a special meaning during lunar flights. The map of the moon's surface has few familiar landmarks for flight controllers to grasp at a glance.

Use of the second color to distinguish special points of importance quickly could be of great help in directing an eventual lunar landing and could be a major factor in the safety of the astronauts.

(For example, during the lunar phase of the Apollo 10 mission an Apollo reference slide showing a lunar map in one color and the primary and secondary landing sites in a second color, will be projected on the 10 × 20-foot screen simultaneously. Real-time information from six other projectors, including predicted and actual lunar orbit trajectories and blips of the tracked Command Module and Lunar Module spacecraft, will be shown in various colors selected by the computer or manually.)

The slides used in Mission Control must meet extreme requirements:

—They must be precise (accuracies within two-ten thousandths of an inch are required).

—They must yield a sharp image even under magnifications of up to 240 times their original size, which is one-half by one inch.

—They must withstand heat of up to 400 degrees Farenheit.

—Their color content must be impervious to heavy concentrations of ultra-violet radiation emitted by the projectors' xenon arc light sources.

Addition of color to the Mission Control Center slide file has implications beyond the space program. The process is adaptable to commercial projection needs any time absolute fidelity is required in combination with extreme magnification or projection over relatively long distances. Uses might occur typically at trade fairs, in convention halls, airports or sports stadiums.

Credit for the color breakthrough is being given to the Manned Spacecraft Center's Precision Slide Laboratory, staffed by Philco-Ford technicians directed by Emmett S. Sweningson.

The same team four years ago successfully produced the first data reference slides for the Mission Control display system—a feat considered by some to be beyond the state-of-the-art.

Working with Mr. Sweningson are Photo Technologist specialists Ray R. Schmidt and Anthony S. Nides and Senior Photo Technologist James W. Cook. Mr. Cook perfected the two-color technique which will be used in Apollo 10. Mr. Schmidt and Mr. Nides are working on advanced techniques which eventually will permit use of the entire spectrum.

Color has been a goal of the Precision Slide Laboratory since April, 1965, when the Mission Operations Control Room projectors had been installed, but no background slides had yet been manufactured.

About a year ago, after several earlier attempts had proven unacceptable, Mr. Cook decided to use a filter approach to coating a slide.

He needed a dye which could be applied to the heat-resistant glass in an even layer of controllable thickness, be compatible with the chemical processes used in other steps of slide production, yet be transparent, have good saturation and be durable under heat and radiation.

One organic dye that appeared to meet all other qualifications lasted only 20 minutes under the UV radiation of the projector lamps. Filtration extended the life of the dye to only 22 minutes. A minimum life of 24 hours was required for the slide to be useful.

In February, 1969, Mr. Cook found a chemical dye with a pigment which met all requirements. Using a map of the lunar surface showing the preferred and alternate landing sites, he prepared test slides which underwent 120 hours of continuous exposure to the heat and UV radiation of the projectors with no apparent color degradation.

On March 14, the day after the Apollo 9 splashdown, flight controllers who will direct Apollo 10 approved use of the new color slides after seeing a demonstration presented by Mr. Sweningson and Mr. Cook.

Mr. Sweningson said the laboratory is working to refine the Cook technique, and to perfect the systems being explored by Mr. Schmidt and Mr. Nides.

In the first paragraph of this release, the main idea is presented. This is that photographic technologists developed the new technique. The second paragraph introduces the second idea which is that the color slides will be used for the first time at NASA's mission control center. The last sentence of the second paragraph gives the third idea, that the technique is adaptable to commercial use.

The third paragraph refers back to the first idea, the development of the technique. The fourth paragraph refers to the second idea, the use of the technique by NASA.

The fifth paragraph is the perspective explanation, which is the same type of section described in a preceding section under the heading of perspective summary lead. In this release, the perspective paragraph presents the problem: the reason for development of the technique.

Paragraph six again refers back to the development of the technique. The seventh through ninth paragraphs talk about the second idea. It is not until the tenth paragraph that the third idea (adaptable to commercial use) is brought in again.

In the rest of the release, the three ideas are developed further.

Composite Structure.   Again, if a release is intended to present more than two or three ideas, the inverted pyramid becomes difficult to handle. There is another type of structure that can be used, called the composite or wrap-up, which is useful in cases in which there are several ideas to be presented that are of approximately equal weight.

The composite structure release is made up of a summary lead and a point-by-point development of the subject. The following is an imaginary case in which the composite structure could be used to good effect.

Ace Manufacturing Company has decided to put together various capabilities from different departments and to enter a new line of business. The new business is health equipment and services. The equipment and capabilities include:

- A fiber optic probe coupled with a television camera which can be used for medical diagnosis. It was originally developed to inspect the inside of small, long, hollow shafts.
- A computer technique for analyzing the flow of materials through a hospital. This was developed as a result of the company's president donating some of his computer expert's time, as a goodwill gesture, in an attempt to reduce the cost of operation of a local hospital.
- A small, inexpensive air pollution measurement device which will be useful to the elderly, those with respiratory problems, and others whom air pollution seriously affects. The device resulted from research on air pollution measurement which Ace did for a large steel company.
- An improved monitor for displaying fluoroscopic pictures. This monitor resulted from work on industrial x-ray inspection machines.

The announcement of Ace's new business aspirations could be handled in a variety of ways. If the Ace publicity man decided to present the total story in one release, a composite structure would be the best way of organizing the story. This would consist of a summary lead followed by sections devoted to the various capabilities. The story might look like the following.

NEW YORK, N. Y., June 12—A new entrant in the medical equipment and services field was announced here today. John A. Smith, president of Ace Manufacturing Corp., said that after an extensive business study, Ace has decided it can profitably pursue this market.

Ace initially will offer four products and services in the new market. These are: a new type of probe for medical diagnosis, a computer technique that will help reduce the cost of hospital operation, an inexpensive home air pollution measurement device, and an improved monitor for fluorscopic pictures.

The fiber optic probe . . .

From there on, the four product and service areas would be described in detail, one after the other.

PRODUCT NEWS RELEASE

The product news story may very well be the most used industrial publicity tool. It is also the type most directly related to the business of a company, in that it is used to help sell products and services. For these reasons, it deserves to be covered in more detail.

A product news release describes a product or service, tells what is good about it, where it is to be used, and where to obtain it. Figures 9-3 and 9—4 are, respectively, examples of product and service announcement releases.

Most business publications carry new product information. In fact, there are a few publications that carry nothing but product information. The rest of the business publications that use product information—and they are in the majority—usually have a section in the back devoted to it. The size of the section varies with the publication's format and editorial purpose. It may be as small as part of a page carrying a few product stories, or it may run from a fourth or a third of the total number of pages to the entire issue as in the type of publication mentioned above that carries product information exclusively.

Editors rely almost entirely on product information supplied by companies and agencies. Other types of material are obtained at least partly through the efforts of the publication's staff, but usually not product information. This means that a company cannot depend upon publications to ferret out this type of material but must provide it to them.

One of the reasons publications rely so heavily on companies for product information is that many companies, especially larger ones, have always provided it in abundance. In fact, most business publications receive far more than they use.

Product releases are therefore both an opportunity and a challenge. They are an opportunity in that business publications want and need them, and a challenge in that they must be more useful than the run-of-the-mill product release in order to be printed.

The product release has a single, clear objective: to help sell something. The main difference between it and most other types of releases is that it contains an unabashed sales message. This being the case, product releases are produced with the active participation of salesmen and marketing executives. This can be a problem, since some marketing men are convinced that, if a company buys space for an advertisement, the publication should be kind enough to run a small product announcement also. The following comments were taken from guides issued by two business publications to help companies in supplying product releases.

School Product News:

> It (a product story) will run or get thrown out on its own merits. Implying that there might be some advertising in the offing (for example, a letter that starts out, "Since yours is one of a group of publications that has been suggested for next year's schedules, I am enclosing an announcement . . .") is an insult to the editor. It puts the kiss of death on your story.

Design News:

> Please don't hint at possible advertising schedules that are being planned for this magazine. Editorial judgement alone determines which new products appear.

Product Features

In the eyes of editors, the ideal product release is one that describes a product that is about to be marketed for the first time, has never been advertised prior to submission of the press release, and is not being announced in other media. Although this ideal is seldom achieved, the thing that comes closest is the product feature.

Some of the more specialized publications use product features. These are treatments that are lengthier and more prominently displayed than the majority of product items carried. Some of the requirements a product feature must meet are the following.

1. The main requirement is that the product feature be a first-use exclusive. This means that the publication to which it is submitted has the opportunity to print the information before any of its competitors. Most editors who use product features do not object to a release being distributed at the same time the product feature appears in their publication. They seldom insist upon a complete exclusive.

2. The product must of course be one needed by readers of the publication.

3. There must be something newsworthy about the product.

4. The information should be accompanied by a good illustration.

Product Release Characteristics

As with other types of releases, newsworthiness is a primary characteristic of product releases. Again, the three interrelated elements, subject, media, and audience, are of paramount importance in the determination of what is newsworthy. And again, the subject is usually an outgrowth of the objective. In the case of a product release, the objective, as previously indicated, is usually simply to sell something. But in order to serve as a vehicle for a sales message, the story must be printed.

If the story has nothing newsworthy about it in terms of the subject, the media, and the audience, it will not be used. Generally, the answer to one of the following questions must be "yes" in order for a product to qualify for product news treatment:

- Is the product really new?
- If not completely new, is the product a substantially improved version of an existing product?

To be typographically complete, a product news release should contain the following format elements.

- A product news designation. This can be in the form of a preprinted letterhead which says something like "product news" or "new product information." It can also be stated or strongly implied in a headline.
- Company name, address, and telephone number.
- Name of someone who can be contacted by letter or telephone for additional information.
- Date on which the release is mailed, a release date, or both.

Most product releases can be prepared by using some variation of the following outline.

1. Lead
   a. Statement of main feature.
   b. Capsule description.
   c. General function.
2. Applications (uses for the product).
3. Operation (how the product works).
4. Performance details.
5. Operating economies.
6. Specifications and data.
   a. Ratings and capacity.
   b. Size and weight.
   c. Interface requirements.
7. Price and availability.
8. Manufacturer—name, address, and telephone, and teletype number.

The following is a typical example of a product release.

NEW TESTER FOR ROTATING ELECTRICAL EQUIPMENT NOW AVAILABLE

A new tester that enables faster, more accurate testing for faults in windings of motors, generators and many types of transformers and electromagnetic coils is now available.

The surge comparison tester is for use in manufacturing, maintenance, and repair of rotating electrical equipment of all sizes. It indicates the presence of faults—shorts, grounds or dissimilarity in number of turns—by comparing the impedance in two identical windings or sections of a winding.

The unit is so sensitive that it will indicate a difference of just one in a number of turns, or a short between one turn and another in even a large winding with hundreds of turns.

The tester delivers a low-energy, high voltage transient to the winding under test, alternating the direction of the voltage every cycle or 60 times per second. The transient delivered by the tester can be from 1 to 10 watts. A typical pusle might be rated at 100 watts and 1 milliampere. Each cycle is presented on a cathode ray tube. If no fault is present, there is only one trace on the cathode ray tube. If a fault causes the impedance between the two windings or winding sections to be different, two different wave forms appear on the cathode ray tube.

All the new unit's controls are on the front panel within easy reach of the operator. Parts under test are protected from unwanted transients by the tester's protective circuitry.

Measuring 21-3/4 inches wide by 22 inches deep by 30 inches high, the two models of the tester weigh respectively 200 pounds for model P/N 976J552-1 and 230 pounds for model P/N 976J552-2.

Power inputs for the two models of the tester are 115 to 125 volts, 60 cycles per second, 7 amperes for P/N 976J552-1 and 220 to 240 volts, 50 cycles per second, 4 amperes for the P/N 976J552-2.

For further information on the new surge comparison tester, contact . . .

Glossy print 27494-30 enclosed.

The release follows the outline given above in most of its particulars. This can be seen from the following comparison.

1. Lead
   a. Statement of main
      feature   "faster, more accurate testing"
   b. Capsule description   "a new tester"
   c. Function   "testing for faults in windings"

2. Applications

"manufacturing, maintenance, and repair of rotating electrical equipment of all sizes"

3. Operation

"It indicates the presence of faults—shorts, grounds or dissimilarity in number of turns—by comparing the impedence in two identical windings or sections of a winding."

"The tester delivers a low-energy, high-voltage transient to the winding under test, alternating the direction of the voltage every cycle of 60 times per second. The transient delivered by the tester varies from 1 to 10 watts. A typical pulse might be rated at 100 volts and 1 milliampere. Each cycle is presented on a cathode ray tube. If a fault causes the impedance between the two windings or winding sections to be different, two different wave forms appear on the cathode ray tube."

4. Performance details

"The unit is so sensitive that it will indicate a difference of just one in a number of turns, or a short between one turn and another in even a large winding with hundreds of turns."

"All the new unit's controls are on the front panel within easy reach of the operator. Parts under test are protected from unwanted transients by the tester's protective circuitry."

5. Operating economics

In this case, the economy is implied. If the tester is faster and more accurate, it will probably provide reduced costs, and interested experts who read the story will recognize these economies.

6. Specifications and data
   a. Ratings and capacities

"60 test pulses per second," "1 to 10 watts, 100 volts at 1 milliamp."

   b. Size and weight

Size: "21¾ inches wide by 22 inches deep by 30 inches high." Weight: 200 pounds for one model and 230 pounds for the other.

c. Interface requirements	Power inputs are "115 to 125 volts, 60 cycles per second, 7 amperes" for one model; "220 to 240 volts, 50 cycles per second, 4 amperes" for the other.
7. Price and availability	The tester described was a specially built unit that was not kept in inventory by the company. Availability varied with the shop load at the time of an order. For these reasons, the company decided to quote availability only to customers at the time they contacted the company. Regarding price, the unit cost varied somewhat with the features requested by different customers.
	Also, the unit cost was quite high and the company's marketing experts decided that they would lose more potential customers by giving the price then by not giving it. The feeling of the marketing men was that, if they had an opportunity to present the advantages of the product directly to customers, they would be able to justify its high price.
8. Manufacturer's name, address, and telephone and teletype numbers	Although omitted from the example, these are normally included in a release.

Special Considerations in Writing Product Releases

In addition to the release writing considerations given earlier in this chapter, there are a few special considerations in the preparation of product releases.

A positive identification of the product must be made as early as possible in the release. If a headline is used, the identification can be made there. Generic terms such as "transistor" or "motor" should be included. When the generic terms are too general, appropriate modifiers can be used. For example, the word "filter" can refer to several things. It should be specified whether the product is an "electronic filter" or an "air filter." Adjectives such as "unique" or "totally new " are not what might be considered appropriate modifiers. Most editors have a passionate dislike for such modifiers. Some even go so far as to say that the word "new" should not be used in a product release, because the very fact that a release is sent out means that the product is new. That, however, is probably putting too fine a point on it.

One reason that product identification is so important is that the sorting or press releases, especially in the case of magazines with large staffs, is done by secretaries or editorial assistants. It should be clear to even an unitiated secretary that the release is a product story. She should be able to recognize the general type or class of product and route the release to the proper editor.

Specialized Terminology

Jargon is often unavoidable and sometimes even desirable in a product story. It can be desirable if the product has a narrow range of application, and if the audience and media are highly specialized. Specialized editors and readers might feel their intelligence is being insulted by material that has been generalized and interpreted to an unnecessary degree.

Jargon should in general be minimized, however. Acronyms and abbreviations should be used sparingly, and carefully spelled out when there is the slightest chance of misinterpretation.

Editing

It is often possible to edit existing material into product releases rather than write them from scratch. It is probably safe to say that the majority of product releases are prepared just that way.

The way this is usually done is to ask an engineer to provide a brief write-up on the features of the product. This can often be edited with very little trouble, especially if the engineer has an understanding of what a product release should contain.

Company Identification

Many, and perhaps most, companies and agencies put the company's name in the headline, the first paragraph or both. Magazines invariably take it out of both places and put it at the end of the story. It is partly a matter of pride and partly of practice to put the name at the beginning of the release. But it does not make sense to do something editors obviously do not like.

Putting the name, address, and telephone number where they belong at the end of the release makes the story easier for the editor to use. He does not have to rewrite the first paragraph.

Product Information Questionaire

Some companies find it useful to prepare a product information question-aire which can be used by the publicity man as a starting point for product releases. This is most useful when the company has a wide variety of products or a product line with many variants. Multiproduct companies generally need a steady flow of product releases as new products and variations of existing products are made available. Moreover, the investment in money and manpower to fulfill the need is usually a bare minimum. So anything that speeds up the publicity production process is helpful. Product information questionnaires can in some cases do this.

A product information questionnaire should be tailored to a particular company or product line. One approach is to use as a starting point the typical product story outline given previously. A questionnaire based on this outline might look like the following.

Name of product:
Main feature:
Capsule description:
General function:
Applications:
Operation:
Performance details:
Operating Economies:
Rating and capacities:
Size and weight:
Interface requirements:
Price:
Availability:
Photos available:
For additional information, contact:

The main problem with this approach is getting everyone concerned to think in the same terms. There is likely to be some confusion about the meaning of such words as function, performance, and operation, especially in relation to each other. People in different industries and companies, and even in different parts of a single company, often have their own definitions for such things. This is why it is essential that a questionnaire be tailored to the particular situation.

Illustrations

Product releases with illustrations result in more coverage than those without. One editor says that product stories with illustrations bring in about double the number of inquiries. He therefore strongly favors releases with illustrations. As pointed out before, a worthwhile objective is to try to send out an illustration with every release.

Some products lend themselves to application photos. That is, photos that show the product being used. If the product is an end item, such as a fork lift or chain saw, application shots can be effective. But if the product is a component, a form of raw material, or a "black box," the application shot is usually not a good idea. For example, a photo of the inside of a television set to illustrate a product story on a resistor would probably not be appropriate. Likewise, in cases of items such as valves, bearings, springs, and other mechanical components, the product is either inaccesible or totally overwhelmed by the thing it is a part of.

In cases in which products do not lend themselves to application photos, there is nothing much that can be done except to supply a stereotyped product shot. Such photos generally do not have a person in them, unless they show a large piece of apparatus or equipment. Relative size is shown in a variety of other ways, most often in comparison with a ruler or coin or some other common thing everyone recognizes.

Even stereotyped product shots should be visually interesting. Good photographers make use of lighting, background, and visual features of the product to create interest in their pictures.

Illustrations do not necessarily have to be photos. Sometimes another type of illustration is better. For example, a product story about a refractory metal alloy might be illustrated better by using a temperature versus tensile strength curve instead of a photo. A schematic diagram might be better for a product story on a miniature electronic circuit or a pneumatic component.

To summarize, some of the important product photo considerations are:

- There should be something in the photo to show relative size. What that might be is limited only by the imaginations of the writer and the photographer.
- The photo should strongly identify the product, so that when a reader sees a much reduced picture in print he can still identify the product and, hopefully, even pick out the distinctive features.
- The photos should of course be of the best technical quality obtainable. They should be sharp, have high contrast, and be well composed.

- The vast majority of product shots are reduced by a considerable amount before printing, and photos should be made with that factor in mind.
- If there is the slightest possibility of someone not knowing which is the top of the photo, the top should be labeled.
- Glossy prints are a requirement, preferably 8 × 10 inches.
- The illustration should never be a screened (halftone) photo. This guarantees that the photo will not be used.
- Attach captions to a photo with rubber cement. Tape is sometimes used; it can damage the print when the caption is removed.
- Photos should be mailed with cardboard stiffeners. If no stiffener is included, a photo will in many cases be cracked, making it unusable.
- Generally, retouching a photo of a product is not a good idea. Such photos resemble advertising and catalog illustrations, and for that reason editors are reluctant to use them.
- The prints mailed to publications should be black and white. Publications seldom use color except for a rare photo inside and occasionally on a cover.

REFERENCES

W. R. Harrison, *Write for Trade Journals*, The Writer, Inc., Boston, Mass., 1949.

Bruce Westley, *News Editing*, Houghton Mifflin, The Riverside Press, Cambridge, Mass., 1953.

13

PRODUCING ARTICLES

Just as Chapter 12 was a more detailed treatment of the producing of press releases, so this chapter describes that part of publicity writing that falls under the category of the article. As a publicity tool, it is second only to the press release in frequency of usage.

A sampling shows that a large number of business publications use signed articles. The information is given in the accompanying table. It was taken from *Bacon's Publicity Checker*, a handbook that gives detailed listings of publications and the types of material they use.

Field	Number Listed	Number Using Signed Articles	Percentage
Chemical industry	51	36	70.5
Electrical and electronic	94	80	85
Industrial	191	88	46
Metal trade	43	42	98
Petroleum	57	49	86
Traffic and warehousing	25	19	76

WRITING CONSIDERATIONS

Objective–Subject–Audience

The objective of an article can run the gamut from the very specific, such as helping to sell a product, to the very general, such as helping to improve a company's stature or reputation. And in many cases, an article has a multifaceted objective or more than one objective. The objective should stem from a plan.

The publicity man may feel an article is needed for reasons that differ entirely from those of the author. But for whatever reasons the article is begun, there is generally one common ingredient: the author has some personal stake in the article. It might be that he does it to help have the product he engineered specified and put into use. At the other extreme, the author does it merely for professional recognition. Between these two ends of the spectrum lie the articles written for more than one reason, to meet more than one objective.

Therefore one characteristic of articles is that the objective or objectives may not be singular or as clear-cut as those of the press release. Another aspect is that authors must have a personal stake in the article; it must meet one of their own objectives before they will even be receptive to the idea of writing it.

To reiterate an idea from Chapter 7 the subject should be an outgrowth of the objective. But there is a greater feedback effect from the subject to the objective in the article than in the press release. This reinforces the notion implied above, that the article objective may not be as specific as that of the press release.

Since most articles are major efforts, authors need major motivations just to get started. This is true whether an article is produced by a publicity writer or by an engineer, scientist, or specialist. This means that, if the objective is weak, the motivation will be weak and the busy prospective author will not be interested in what apparently is unimportant work.

One thing all this shows is that the signed article as a publicity tool is generally more difficult to manage than the press release. But within its bounds, the article is extremely useful. As previously noted, the article commands enough space to explain something in detail. This makes it possible to present a point or points that may otherwise be hard to put across. Another advantage noted is that the article has an extremely high degree of credibility.

In addition to the objective and the subject, another major consideration is the audience which consists of the media and the readers.

All these considerations are interrelated. Figure 13-1 is a simple flow diagram which shows the relationships for most articles. It illustrates the role of feedback in the process, and points up the importance of continual rethinking and adjustment as the article production process proceeds.

Chronologically, an objective gives rise to a subject which is the direct cause of the article. The article is published and, hopefully, read. If the process works properly, the idea embodied by the objective winds up in the minds of a desired set of readers.

The needs of the readers, which in turn become the needs of the publications that serve the readers, primarily determine the acceptability of

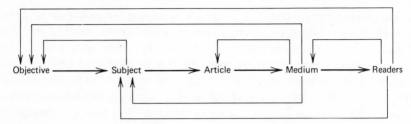

Figure 13-1. Article flow diagram.

an article. There are, however, a large number of other elements that influence acceptability. The flow chart shows that of all the elements involved only the article itself is concrete and objective. Everything connected with it is abstract and subjective. Some of these subjective elements are the originating plan, the objective of the article, the motivation for the article, the subject (at least until the article is written), the selection of a publication at which to aim the article, and the acceptance or rejection of the article by an editor. Because of this high degree of subjectivity, nothing can be considered anywhere near settled until an editor accepts a manuscript for publication.

It is not quite enough to indentify reader's needs. It is also important to establish whether or not these needs can be fulfilled, and whether or not there is a publication to fulfill them. Although this can usually be quickly settled by a little thought, it is a consideration important enough to add to the list.

A certain type of reader need is fulfilled by business publications geared to improving day-to-day work or to solving immediate problems. There is also an element, which varies in strength from publication to publication, of professional improvement, but this is usually a secondary role. The latter is generally left to society-sponsored journals which are more tutorial in nature. The reason business publications concentrate on immediate help for the reader is that this attracts readers more strongly. Publications for profit must of course attract readers to stay in business.

Needs of readers involve such things as problems in design, production, and supervision of employees; reducing expenses; increasing sales, profits, and efficiency; keeping abreast of trends, changes, new developments in the industry, and the economy; and competitive information.

Information to help meet the needs of readers can be broken down into technology information and intelligence. Information dealing mainly with methods and equipment generally falls in the technology category. Some of the elements mentioned above that come under this heading are problems in design, production, and supervision; reducing expenses; and increasing sales, profits, and efficiency. The elements that come under intelligence are trends, changes, new developments, opportunities, and competitive information.

The technology-versus-intelligence breakdown is a useful viewpoint, especially in the early stages of article production. The majority of the publications that use signed articles are in the technology information category, and the main vehicle they use—at least in terms of amount of editorial space—to convey such information is the signed article. This is not to say that it is the only vehicle, for they use news columns, unsigned features, and product information as well.

The technology category includes a huge number of business publications, one or more in every industry, discipline, field, or specialization, no matter how narrow. Some publications cover only a narrow specialization, others cut across specializations or industries. Technology publications probably all have magazine formats.

The field is narrowed by the article objective and the writer's own expertise. And in most cases, he has in mind the magazine he can write for. Even if the prospective author is relatively sure which magazine to aim for, it still does not hurt to do a little checking. Browsing in the library is one way. Another is to dip into *Bacon's Publicity Checker* and *Business Publications Rates and Data*. Most public relations and advertising people have these publications, or have access to them.

The main advantage of *Bacon's Publicity Checker* is that it tells whether or not publications use signed articles. Also, there are clues about the nature of publications that can be gleaned from Bacon's volume. For one thing, it gives circulation figures and frequency of publication. For another, it tells which publications charge for cuts. This means that when the publication decides to use a publicity photo it has received from a company or agency, it bills the sender for the cost of having an engraving or printing negative made. Publicity people usually have little respect for publications that charge for cuts. Whether that is always justified has not been established. But most people in industry and agencies feel that it is at best a questionable practice.

Business Publications Rates and Data does not tell whether or not publications use signed articles, but it has more information on readers than just the circulation figures. It gives the distribution of readers by job classification and by geographical distribution. It also details the type of editorial information that publications use.

The final determination of which publication or publications should be selected can realistically be made only by looking at the publications themselves. In addition to finding out whether or not they use signed articles, the publications should be reviewed for other reasons. Foremost among these are the nature of the readership, editorial relevance, and editorial requirements.

The author may feel that he knows what the readers are looking for, since he may be a reader of the magazines he is considering. There is a good chance, however, that he is not a typical reader. He therefore needs to go through this step, keeping in mind the point of it all, which is to determine to whom the magazines are aimed, as he scans the editorial, news columns, letters to the editor, advertisements, articles, and product and literature sections.

The second thing mentioned as something to look for in magazines is editorial relevance. The main question concerns how well the publication serves its readers. Some magazines that were very readable, superbly edited, and put together in a highly pleasing fashion have gone out of business in the last few years, while some that were less well done have survived. So editorial relevance should not be confused with the apparent quality of the final product.

The other important thing to look for in reviewing magazines is the editorial purpose or policy, which is what determines the editorial requirements. Some of these requirements are timeliness, value to readers, degree of specialization, length, type of articles, handling and type of illustrations, and use of references.

Many business publications provide guides for prospective authors. If there is time, these can be requested. Also, companies or agencies sometimes have a file of such guides.

The Article Process

Three phases in the article process can be identified. These can be called the selling, writing, and manuscript placement and handling phases. They can be chronologically diagrammed as follows.

Writing ① Phase	② Selling Phase	③ Manuscript Placement and Handling Phase
Research	Publication selection	Submission
Outline	Query	Acceptance or rejection and re-
Gestation	Expression of interest by	submission
Drafting	an editor	Preparation of an edited version
Revision	Determination of editorial	Checking of edited version
	requirements	Checking of galley or page proofs
		Layout and finalization

The selling phase is made up of the selection of a publication, the query, obtaining an indication of an editor's interest in the subject, and determining the magazine's requirements.

The writing phase consists of research outlining, gestation, drafting the manuscript, and revising the manuscript.

Manuscript placement and handling involves submission, acceptance, or rejection and resubmission, preparation of an edited version by a magazine, checking of the edited version by the author, and checking of galley or page proofs (usually by the editor, sometimes by the author, and in some instances in lieu of checking an edited version), and layout and finalization by the magazine.

The selling phase is partly concurrent with the writing phase. After the outline is prepared, the selling phase can be started. This may continue through the gestation stage and into the drafting stage. The author should, however, wait for the determination of editorial requirements before he puts the manuscript in final form.

Establishing a dialogue with an editor by sending him a query is always a good idea. However, more often than not, this step is omitted. Whatever their reasons, engineers and other technologists often prefer to complete an article rather than go through the process of outlining, submitting the outline, waiting for a response, and then writing the article. The way one magazine encourages queries is the example in Figure 9-10.

Acceptance is the major milestone in the life of an article. But even though it is the major hurdle, acceptance is still not an absolute quarantee that the article will be published. Editors may change their minds or be replaced, editorial policies may change, and business conditions may vary.

Article Production Methods

The three most common article production methods are writing from scratch, adapting papers and reports, and ghostwriting.

In writing an article from scratch, the person whose signature or by-line will appear on the article when it is published does nearly all the work, from formulating the idea to writing to assembling illustrations. He may receive some assistance from a technical writing group in the form of editing, and a drafting group may help with illustrations. But with this method, the author does the majority of the work and he is closely involved with the rest of it, such as editing or illustration preparation.

Adapting papers and reports is the second most common way articles are produced. Papers that have been presented before an organization become the "property" of the organization. There is a large grey area surrounding the question of what constitutes ownership and exactly what it is that is owned. The thing to remember is that it is unethical and probably illegal to submit a paper for publication by a magazine other than its so-called owner, especially if the editor is not told that the paper has been presented.

A paper can be used as the *basis* of an article, however, and is considered acceptable as an article if it is substantially changed. It is important to note, though, that papers are generally written for different purposes and in a somewhat different format than articles. So a paper usually needs a large amount of revision before it becomes an acceptable article.

Ghostwriting can be considered the third major article production method. In this case someone other than the person whose name is in the by-line does most or all of the work involved. Sometimes the ghost writer's name appears as coauthor of the article. This happens when a manager or supervisor asks one or more of his subordinates to collaborate on an article with him. The subordinate actually winds up writing most of the article and assembling data and illustrations, because the boss is usually too busy to do much of the time-consuming detail work on an article.

Sometimes the writer is a specialist in ghosting who is brought in and paid to do the article. Editors of magazines sometimes write articles from information provided to them by the company, and put the signature of someone from the company on it. They may do this when it seems impossible to the editor that they will be able to find anyone in the company to write the article. Of course, the subject must be very significant to make the editor want an article badly enough to do it himself.

Ghost writers are sometimes employed by publicity people. To be honest, most of them feel they are not capable of writing articles. They do not believe they are technically qualified, or do not have the amount of writing experience required to write a specialized article in some field other than their own.

Manuscript Elements

There are several manuscript elements that are conventionally used. It is simpler and more understandable for everyone concerned if a standard format is followed.

Manuscripts should be typed of course, and should be double spaced. If possible, a typed original should be supplied to a magazine, never a poor office machine copy or a carbon copy. Occasionally, a company makes quality reproductions of a manuscript for its internal approval process. If the reproduction is as legible as the typed original, or almost so, the reproduction can be submitted.

The material should be typed on one side of the page. The pages should be the standard 8 1/2 × 11 inches.

The text should begin a half or a third of the way down the first page.

This is to allow the editor to write in his own title and his printing instructions.

A title should be included. Even though the magazine will probably write its own, a title is helpful because it gives the editor a hint as to the content when he begins to review the article.

The by-line or signature should follow the title. It is usually given in this form:

> John R. Smith
> Chief Engineer
> Acme Tool Company
> New York, N.Y.

Wherever possible, a summary lead should begin the article. Some highly specialized subjects, however, do not lend themselves to this treatment. The summary lead is useful to an editor in two ways. First, it gives him a better idea as to what the article is about. Second, it might be the basis of a "blurb." Many magazines have gone to the blurb or subheadline treatment in which a capsule description is set in type smaller than the headline, but larger than the type of the article proper. Some magazines use the blurb in lieu of a summary lead; some use both blurb and summary lead.

Subheadings may or may not appear in the article. They are usually thought to be the responsibility and domain of the editor. However, subheadings are helpful to the editor in understanding long and highly specialized articles. The editor needs all the help he can get along this line, especially with articles that are not particularly well written—a category many if not most articles fall into.

Paragraphs should be as short as possible. Overly long paragraphs are often a sign that the writer has gone too far into detail without referring to the point he is trying to make—one way of losing the reader.

As pointed out in Chapter 11, pieces of writing must be broken into units. These are usually, and ideally, paragraphs, but may be multiparagraph units. Each unit should have an opening sentence, called the topic sentence, which summarizes the unit.

A means of identifying the second and succeeding pages of the manuscript should be included. This can take the form of the author's last name at the top left of each page.

The pages should of course be numbered.

An acknowledgment paragraph is included at the end of some articles. This gives credit to others in the field who have helped the author, directly or indirectly, or who have made significant contributions to the field and have not received acknowledgment for them.

The acknowledgment should be included only if it is necessary to give highly deserved credit. In other words, credit sections should not be used just for the sake of having one at the end of the article.

A list of references is a part of most articles. These references may or may not be cited in the text by numbers, such as by superscript, or may just be listed in case readers want additional information on the subject.

Lists of illustrations should be used for articles that have a lot of illustrations. Each item on a list of illustrations should include a figure number and a brief caption or legend indicating what the illustration is (diagram, chart, photo, schematic) and giving enough of an explanation to enable the editor to determine where it is to be used in the article. The illustrations themselves should have figure numbers noted on them.

Footnotes are infrequently used in articles, since editors usually prefer to include all the information in the text of the article.

Most authors worry about length. Editors in general do not make strict length limitations. In most cases they prefer to say that an article should be as long as necessary but no longer. Even so, they consider brevity a cardinal virtue.

Writing Quality

The subjects of readability and clarity are covered in some detail in Chapter 11. Beyond that, however, there is one element of writing quality that is a special problem in article writing. This is obscurity. Much has been written about the apparent inability of scientists, engineers, and other professionals and specialists to write plainly and understandably.

Various reasons for this problem have been offered. Colleges and universities are blamed for not doing a good job of teaching the subject of writing. The subconscious fear of exposing oneself to scrutiny has also been suggested. Even the government has been blamed because of its increasing influence and the bureaucratic impersonality and rigidity of its communications.

Whatever the reasons for the unclear and turgid prose, it nevertheless is a problem. F. Peter Woodford, a professor and editor of a scientific journal, writing in an article in which he described obscure writing and some of its effects, said: "You can't get away from it: execrable writing like this is the product of shoddy thinking, of careless condensation, or of pretentiousness."

Even though editors of business publications are concerned mainly with content and secondarily with the quality of writing, article writers cannot ignore the writing quality aspect. Obscurity—and poor organization and sloppy manuscripts—are irritants to editors. In the case of an article that is marginal in content, writing quality can mean the difference between acceptance and rejection. Editors never have enough time to do as much editing as they would like to do. And since they do not run articles that are not up to their standards of clarity and readability, the marginal article that requires much editing is often rejected.

There is another side of the coin of writing quality, however. Alfred North Whitehead said, "Insistence on clarity at all costs is based on sheer superstition as to the mode in which human intelligence functions." This is in keeping with Whitehead's axiom for scientific inquiry that says that everything should be made as simple as possible but no more so. Another way of looking at the problem is suggested by Emberger and Hall in *Scientific Writing*: "The scientific writer has an obligation to his material as well as to the reader." Although most writers of articles for business publications are not scientists, the idea applies to other specializations and professions as well.

This seems to leave the writer in a dilemma. But once again the key is a good understanding of the audience, and the subject in relation to the audience.

Another problem not unique but yet important in article writing is the use of jargon. Nelson Algren gave an excellent explanation of jargon in *Notes from a Sea Diary: Hemingway All the Way*. He gave an example of a review by a critic, and followed it with this passage:

> This is jargon: its 'Yes' is not 'Yes'; its 'No' is not 'No'. It is jargon because it diffuses meaning in order to conceal, rather than reveal, the writer's thought. It is jargon because it conveys the impression the writer is employing Elegant English at the same time it enables him to falsify his thought. It is jargon because it seeks to make an idea, that is easily refutable, irrefutable.

Emberger and Hall draw a useful distinction between shop talk and jargon. They define shop talk as "laboratory or office slang or colloquial usage characteristic of a professional or business group." Jargon, as they see it, is "writing which is unnecessarily pretentious, verbose and involved."

Some use of shop talk is probably unavoidable in business publications. How and what kind a writer can get by with again depend on the audience and the subject in relation to the audience.

WRITING PROCESS

One way of identifying the steps in the article process is to break it into work plan, research, outlining, and drafting the manuscript.

Work Plan

It is important to use an organized approach to the task of writing an article. The writer must deal with a large number of bits of information. He must classify the bits, and group them according to unambiguous relationships. A sequence for an organized approach to a lengthy, complicated article might be the following:

- Research.
- Outline.
- Sectionalize.
- Outline by section.
- Write, section by section.
- Modify overall outline as sections are written.
- Write illustration list giving illustration numbers.
- Write list of references.
- Edit draft.
- Final typing.

In addition to the organized approach, there is another important element of a work plan: budgeting of time to do the research and to write the manuscript. A certain amount of time, either in concentrated form or spread out over a period, must be allocated. Some writers set aside an hour a day, some take a half day a week, and some devote several days exclusively to the job and do it all in a rush. Whatever method suits the individual author, it is essential that time be set aside. It is remarkably easy to procrastinate when writing an article; time budgeting helps get around this almost universal human tendency.

The work plan should also include sources for information, illustration, and typing.

Research

It is probably safe to say that anyone who sets out to write an article for a business publication already knows how to do research. One common research method people in specialized work use is to collect information over a long period of time with the purpose in mind of using it some day to write an article or book.

Writing time for an article is far less than the time spent in research. But for most people, research is much more fun. Still, at some point, the research phase must end.

Outlining and Gestation

Most professional writers say that a fallow period is essential after they have completed their research and before they begin writing. The outline should be completed or revised at the beginning of this period. The time lapse should be a day or more, but even a few hours help a great deal. The writer occupies himself with something other than the article during gestation. When he returns to the task and actually begins writing, he finds it comes much easier and everything hangs together better.

An outline may not be necessary if the article is short and uncomplicated. An example of such an article is one on the design of a simple electronic circuit. However, long and detailed articles—for example, one on renovating a blimp hangar to make a factory—should be carefully outlined. The writer can usually keep the elements of a short and uncomplicated article sorted out in his mind, but this is not always true in the case of the extensive article.

The starting point for an outline is a statement of a purpose or a theme. In reference to the example of the circuit design article, the purpose might be simply to show other engineers how to design a particular electronic circuit in a way that gives improved performance. It is doubtful that anyone would ever take the trouble to spell this purpose out, but then there is really no need to do so. It is simple and straightforward, and the writer most likely would not go off on a tangent for lack of a statement of purpose. However, if the purpose of an article is less obvious, it can be of help to state it. In the example of converting a hangar to a factory, the purpose of an article might be more subtle than simply to tell how such a conversion is made. Instead, it might be to tell how to make use of air-conditioning equipment in converting an existing building into a factory.

As pointed out in Chapter 12, there are two basic types of outlines, the topical and the expository. The topical form is the classic outlining method taught in English composition. The expository is a form in which the subject is broken into its logical parts and each part is summarized. Such an outline might consist of three paragraphs, each representing a section of the article, or it might be several paragraphs long.

An outlining method that can be termed sectionalizing is an approach to article writing often useful to people in industry. It is analagous to the manufacturing of a complicated piece of equipment. On the assembly line, the job is broken into many small tasks which are for the most part done sequentially. The equipment is built up from components to subassemblies to assemblies to a finished product.

An article can be considered to consist of components which are sentences, subassemblies which are paragraphs, assemblies which are sections, all put together according to a good design which is the outline.

The various parts of the equipment, and of an article, must be integrated, as they say in shop talk. In the article, this integration is the transition. To the extent possible, paragraphs should be written so they interlock. One paragraph or one section should naturally lead into the next. Just as equipment should do its job smoothly with all its parts operating together, so an article must read smoothly with no gaps or confusing breaks where transitions should be.

Organization

Of the many methods of organization, or ways of looking at organization, two are most often used for signed articles for business publications. These can be thought of as chronological and descriptive.

Chronological organization is keyed to sequential events. It is usually a narrative telling how something is done and what happened in each of the sets of sequential events.

The chronological form of organization tells the story by unfolding events and, as such, largely leaves the reader to draw his own conclusions. The descriptive form has more of an ingredient of interpretation in which the author explains something rather than just revealing it.

In the simplest form of descriptive organization, and one widely used, the subject is summarized in the opening one to three paragraphs and then explained in detail in the rest of the article. This is the type of article described in Chapter 11, which has only an opening and a body but no end part or conclusions. Also, it usually does not have a perspective type of introduction. The summary opening gets right into the subject.

Many articles are combinations of the chronological and descriptive forms. Some others defy classification, but are successful in putting the story across.

Finally, the organizational approach that is best depends on the familiar combination of the subject and the audience.

Drafting the Article

The writing of the article has to be done with the audience in mind. The writer has to prove by what he puts on paper that his subject is worth reading about. He has to prove it first to the editor to whom the article will be submitted, and also the the reader.

The first draft should be done primarily to put the information down. In this stage, the writer should not worry much about grammar, jargon, and exact wording. He should write mainly to get the ideas he has in mind ordered and on paper. The draft should be written at one sitting if at all possible. This can usually be easily done in the case of a short article. If the article is long, it usually can be broken into sections and written a section at a time.

Allowing an article to grow section by section has another important advantage. It is an effective way of getting around the psychological block that often prevents writers from starting a large writing job.

The first draft is the big hurdle, and once it is completed the rest is relatively easy. The first draft should be edited or revised at least once. The aim is to make the article as readable and understandable as possible. Here again, the audience has to be kept in mind.

Writers often give their drafts to people they work with to get another viewpoint. It can be extremely useful to have someone else's opinions about a piece of writing. The writer is so close to the subject while he is working on the draft that he may not be able to see the forest for the trees.

When a writer does give his draft to someone else for review, he should tell them for whom the article is intended and the overall purpose or objective.

Since the writer gives his draft to someone else for criticism, that is what he should expect to get. Although he is justifiably proud of what he has accomplished, he should not expect to be uncritically praised.

Illustrations

In business publications, illustrations serve two main purposes. The first is to support the text and the second is to add eye appeal to the publication's pages.

Diagrams, graphs, and photographs supplement and clarify written material. They are often the only way to put some point across. In addition, they can be used to conserve space.

In presenting numerical information, diagrams and graphs are better than tables because they are easier to understand.

Publications generally prefer to have people in photos of equipment that accompany articles. This does two things: It adds human interest to the page, and it provides an excellent size reference.

Photos should be in the form of 8 × 10-inch glossy prints and should have good contrast.

Most business publications prefer to draw their own diagrams and graphs. A small minority ask companies to supply reproducible artwork. In

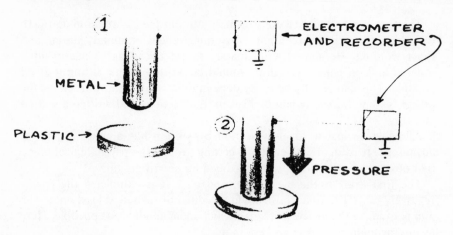

Figure 13-2.   Sketch.

general, it is a good idea to start with good sketches—such as that shown in Figure 13-2—from which the publication can work if it wants to draw its own. If they expect the company to supply the final artwork, they request it; the submission of sketches initially will not cause rejection of the article.

REFERENCES

Bacon's Publicity Checker, 18th ed., Bacon's Publishing Co., Inc., Chicago, Ill., 1969.

R. H. Dodds, *Writing for Technical and Business Magazines*, John Wiley & Sons, Inc., New York, N.Y., 1969.

M. R. Emberger, M. R. Hall, *Scientific Writing*, Harcourt, Brace, and Company, New York, N.Y., 1955.

W. R. Harrison, *Write for Trade Journals*, The Writer, Inc., Boston, Mass., 1949.

H. B. Jacobs, *Writing and Selling Non-Fiction*, Writer's Digest, Cincinnati, Ohio, 1967.

H. M. Patterson, *Writing and Selling Feature Articles*, Prentice-Hall, Inc., Englewood Cliffs, N.J., 1956.

F. Peter Woodford, "Sounder Thinking Through Clearer Writing," *Science*, May 12, 1967, Volume 156, Number 3776, p. 744.

INDEX